God Happened To Be In The Neighborhood

God Bless You —

Ken Young

Prov. 3:5, 6

God Happened
To Be In The
Neighborhood

Ken Jones

VICTOR BOOKS

A DIVISION OF SCRIPTURE PRESS PUBLICATIONS INC.
USA CANADA ENGLAND

Copyediting: Linda Holland
Cover Design: Scott Rattray

Library of Congress Cataloging-in-Publication Data

Jones, Ken, 1946–
　　God happened to be in the neighborhood / by Ken Jones.
　　　p.　cm.
　　ISBN: 1-56476-028-6
　　1. Meditations. 2. Jones, Ken, 1946–　　. I. Title.
BV4832.2.J645　1992　　　　　　　　　　　　　92-15399
242–dc20　　　　　　　　　　　　　　　　　　　　　CIP

1　2　3　4　5　6　7　8　9　10　Printing/Year　96　95　94　93　92

CONTENTS

To Randee
My godly wife and best friend

ACKNOWLEDGMENTS

God has blessed my life with incredible family and friends, and I would like to thank some of them for their contributions in making this book possible.

Thank you . . .

Randee, Marcus, Nathan, and Simeon: The four people who know me best and love me anyway. No husband could have a better encourager; no dad could have three finer sons. Thank you for permission to tell your stories.

Ken and Mary Lou Jones and Jacob and Helen Smith: When God was thinking of the greatest gift He could give to children, He created parents. When God was thinking of the greatest parents He could give to me, He created you.

Dr. Ward Tanneberg, Senior Pastor of Valley Christian Center: Working alongside you every day is a privilege. Thank you for your friendship and allowing me the flexibility of time to write this book.

Pastors and Staff of Valley Christian Center: Your wisdom and spiritual insights bring encouragement to me every day. Dixie, Earl, John, Mark, Nancy, Roger, Steve—my fellow staff pastors—I count you my dearest friends.

Ben and Judy Allen: You've read every word (some of them more than once) and given invaluable comments and corrections. I cherish your friendship.

George and Susan Schmidt: Unselfishly sharing your lovely home in Tahoe made finishing this manuscript more enjoyable and inspiring. You blessed and encouraged me when I needed it.

Jean Dunn: Great secretaries have the gift of knowing when to speak and when to listen. You are a great secretary, and your gift did not go unnoticed.

Kyle Duncan: On a rainy afternoon at Mount Hermon Christian Writer's Conference, you encouraged me to write this book. Your kindness in sharing the manuscript with another editor was unselfish—like Jesus. Thank you.

Linda Holland: Holding the hand of this first-time author and leading me through the maze of publication can't be easy. Your faith in this project, editorial skill, and personal words of encouragement were deeply appreciated.

F.O.C.A.S. (Fellowship of Christian Adult Singles): Thanks for letting me be your pastor. It's an incredible honor.

Ken Jones has written his first book — and it's anointed. I know, because it made me cry. I'm not talking about tears of sadness or pain or regret. I'm talking about tears of recognition.

We rush along in our daily activities and simply miss much of what's happening in our own neighborhood. Ken somehow sees it. He has the lovely knack of looking at common, otherwise ordinary events from a different perspective.

This collection of Ken's stories will make you feel good about your life and all the people in it. But you'd better have a box of tissues handy.

Don't say I didn't warn you.

Pat Boone
Beverly Hills, California

Come walk with me, friend, through the pages of this little book, and I'll show you around my neighborhood; places I've lived, people I've met, and things I've seen. This is a book about neighborhoods—mine and yours—and the people who live in them; a book about life and death and hope and love. It's a book of stories.

It's also a book about God—mine and yours— and the fact that since the beginning, when He walked in the Garden with Adam and Eve, He has chosen to make His abode in the neighborhood of man. I see Him nearly every day, in a variety of settings. He walks the streets; He stands on the corners. He smiles as children make their way to school and rides with commuters on their way to work. He listens to laughter; He cries at funerals. But most of all, I think He yearns.

God has always had a dear and eternal yearning for us to know Him. His desire for a relationship with us is so eternal—His love so long and wide, deep and high—that He sent His Son to stroll the corridors of earth to live and die for us.

I hope that opening the pages of this book will

be like opening a love letter. God's in love. And every morning, with grace upon grace, and mercy upon mercy, He writes to the world: "I love you. Will you be My bride?" Every day, walking through my neighborhood and yours, he writes expressions of His deep love—telling one person at a time, one story at a time, one life at a time—"I love you."

May your heart's door be open to His knock today. Good Neighbor that He is, I can't help thinking He'd love to sit down for a cup of tea with you and me every day, so we can get to know Him better.

·

THE BOOK

WE ARE A FAMILY of musings and stories and books. In fact, I come from a long line of storytellers. Some people talk with their hands. Some people talk with their eyes. I have to talk with my stories. Without my stories, I fumble for things to say. I struggle to communicate. But with stories, musings, "first-person-happenings-to-me," I am freed from the need to think in words, and I can communicate in pictures drawn with sights and sounds and smells. I guess that's why I love to write.

I should not have been surprised, I suppose, when Marcus approached me. He was seven.

"Dad, I think I'm gonna write a book." I pulled the paper I was reading down below the horizon of my eyes and looked full into the face of my son, the budding seven-year-old author. I smiled and said, "Good idea, but we'll have to have some guidelines. Writers always work with guidelines." I could tell by his expression that his seven-year-old mind struggled with the meaning of *guidelines,* but the context didn't give him a clue.

I said, "Guidelines are rules. You can't do your writing on little slips of paper or brown lunch bags and expect to get anywhere. You need to be organized and prepared. I'll make the guidelines for you, OK?" He was obviously thrilled with my acceptance of the idea of his book and readily agreed.

"These are your guidelines," I said. "I will buy a book of blank pages and you fill it with words and ideas and thoughts. A real book with lots of pages will make writing easier for you, and you can keep everything together. The only other guideline is that when you're finished with the book, I get to keep it until you're old enough to care for it yourself." My proposal seemed reasonable to him, and together we started out the door to pick up a blank journal.

After dinner that night, as I sat reading in the living room, Marcus approached me and said he wanted to begin writing right away. "Could I have my book now?" I nodded, and he went to find his mother, who dispensed all household treasures. She handed him a new pencil and the journal we had purchased. He disappeared into his bedroom lair.

He came back ten minutes later, tears filling his eyes. It was obvious he had come upon some terrible disaster. He stood next to me, wishing I would notice. I obliged.

"What's the trouble, little buddy?"

"Nothin'." A hide-and-seek answer inviting me to come and find him. I played the game.

"Come on pal. What's the trouble?"

Now the tears were bigger, and the wells of his eyes were too full to serve as a reservoir. As drops rolled down his face, he said, "O Dad; I can't think of anything to write in this stupid book!" An honest admission. (More authors would do well to be so transparent.)

I picked him up and put my arms around him. We just rocked for a while before I started talking.

"You have to understand something as a writer. Writing a book is not like going to the store and buying a loaf of bread. It's a lot of hard work."

That answer was a start for him, but I knew this conversation was not finished yet. He turned his head and looked in my direction. "How do those guys who write good books do it?" he said. He knew I would know the answer. I didn't write books for a living, of course. I was a pastor. But I was also his dad, and when you're seven years old, daddys know everything (or have to act like they do!).

I said, "Well, they don't just sit down and start in without thinking. Good writing takes a lot of good thinking. Sometimes you have to get off in a corner somewhere ... and just sit ... and think. Then, if a great idea comes to you, you write it down."

We rocked for another ten minutes or so, talking about cats and kites and "Can we go get some ice cream" sorts of things before he finally got off my lap and I went back to my reading.

I glanced over several minutes later to see my seven-year-old pulling an overstuffed chair up to the fireplace. After moments of struggle, he turned and sat down in the chair, placing his feet on the hearth next to the fire, hoping heat and inspiration would transfer from sole to soul. Here was one deep in thought. He felt a book coming on, but before he could write it, he had to think.

After a few reflective moments, he was back in his room — short, young fingers wrapped around a brand new pencil with an unused eraser — printing short, young words, reflecting deeply profound seven-year-old thoughts.

Marcus is twenty-one years old now, and I still have that journal. Some day, I'll give it to him, so he can remember what it was like to be seven years old.

Unless you write books for a living, my guess is

that you haven't given any thought to writer's block this week. Since you probably have no intentions of ever writing a book, it may have been months or even years since you pulled your life up to a fireplace. That's tragic, because everyone is a budding author, whether they know it or not. The Apostle Paul said to the Corinthians, "You are living epistles, known and read by men." You're not writing a book. Your life *is* a book. While you read the words of my life, someone else reads the words of yours. All of us spend hours every day in life's library, reading and being read, watching and being watched.

It really doesn't matter if you're seven or seventy. Writing a good book is not like going to the store and buying a loaf of bread. We would all do well to crawl humbly into the Lap of Heaven more often, and say: "Dad, I can't think of anything to write in this book." Then, look around . . . find a fireplace . . . pull up a chair . . . and think.

It's all too obvious that really great literature is hard to come by these days, and we owe it to ourselves and to God to be the best we know how to be. Nobody likes to read a boring book.

"As iron sharpens iron, so one man sharpens another."
Proverbs 27:17

21

KEEPING IT SIMPLE

TODAY, I HAVE a fantastic opportunity. As I sit at my computer, looking at a blank screen, the cursor blinks benignly and awaits my signal to begin. I can express my ideas with grandiose words and magnanimous articulation. I can write big words on this page, words like *thoroughfare* or *boulevard* or *promenade.*

Or I can keep it simple and use *road.*

I can type thoughts that are abstruse and profound. I can say, "His perspectives are cogitative, filled with sagacity."

Or I can say, "I like the way he thinks."

This computer doesn't care if I use words like *epicurean* or *gastronomic.* It will respond to what I type. I can say, "The last twenty-four hours have been invigorating, gratifying, and absolutely Promethean in every way."

Or, "It's been a good day!" I get to choose.

Good writing and good living are a lot alike.

Every morning, I face a blank page of life, another blinking cursor. I can perambulate through the happenings of today, contemplating the quintessence of their significance.

Or, I can walk in faith. The choice is mine.

I can pendulate and vacillate and bifurcate myself into spiritual schizophrenia.

Or, I can trust and serve and believe.

Simple *is* better. The more profound I try to be — the more ostentatious and ubiquitous my approach to God — the farther I get from the little children Jesus said I need to be like. They use short, easy words to talk to God. They pray for lost kittens. They ask honest, innocent questions like, "Why are our tongues wet?" They reach out in simple faith and hold on to a hand much bigger than their own and assume, "He must know where we're going."

The songwriter got up one morning and sat looking at a blank piece of paper. I can almost picture him leaning back, looking up into the sky and smiling, as a profound thought crossed his mind. He put pen to paper and began the first verse: *"This is the day that the Lord has made; I will rejoice and be glad in it."* Short and simple. Kind of like a blinking cursor on a blank computer screen.

And every day, we get to try it again.

THE GARBAGE LADY

CLARA DIED YESTERDAY. I saw her for the first time several months ago while we were visiting relatives in her hometown. I had heard about her before, but the sight was more than I expected. The locals called her the "Garbage Lady."

She couldn't get inside her house, because it was full of garbage. Piles stood six-to-eight-feet high in every room. Her front door stood open, like a silent sentry, unable to be closed because of the rubble. Garbage cluttered her entire front porch. In fact, the porch was more than cluttered, much more. It was totally covered with tin cans, empty boxes, old rags, and the residue of years of living. Garbage spilled over the sides of the porch, like a cascading waterfall of filth that ran into the yard and filled it too. Clara sat on top of one particular heap—five feet high—like a cherry atop a grotesque sundae made of giant scoops of garbage.

There was a blackness that surrounded that house, a sadness that surrounded that little eighty-year-old lady. And life all around her walked on by, trying not to notice the stench of it all.

Day or night, rain or shine, summer or winter, she could be found sitting in her front yard, covered with a thin sheet of plastic. She busied herself by feeding the hundred-or-so cats that called her house their own private dump. Frequently, she would talk about why she could not go back into her house; some unmentionable event that caused her to fear its safety. "Aren't you afraid out here in the dark and cold?" a passerby would ask. "Yes," she'd reply. "I'm very often afraid. But I can't go back inside." She didn't spend days or weeks sitting in the midst of that squalor and filth—she spent years.

Every morning, a kind neighbor would bring coffee to her, and local residents would walk by and wave and speak. But no one took the responsibility to clean up Clara's garbage. After all, it's a free country, and if you want to sit on a pile of garbage for the rest of your life . . . well. . . . And yesterday *was* the rest of Clara's life. That kindly neighbor brought over the coffee and found her wrapped in her thin sheet of plastic, surrounded by her cats; a lifeless form atop a mound of garbage. Hypothermia and exposure to the elements were listed as the cause of death. But the truth is, she never learned to deal with the garbage.

I saw *him* again this morning. In fact, I look into his face every morning as I shave. Thinking about that garbage lady made me wonder how *he* was doing at taking out the garbage in *his* life. I wondered how many people walk by his life every day and wish he'd do something about his anger or resentment or pride. I wondered how many rooms in his life were unavailable to him because unresolved issues stand in the doorway like a silent sentry. What fears and insecurities keep him from God's very best for his life?

Garbage is a by-product of living. And I can either acknowledge that much of the time, life is a bunch of garbage — and grow — or wrap myself in a plastic facade, climb atop my personal pile of life's inequities, and die spiritually.

The difference between the two is the difference between the smell of the city dump and the smell of a beautiful rose . . . fertilized with a compost heap.

FOURTH-GRADERS

AND NOW, I WILL tell you about family.

We have three sons. Marcus is the oldest, then Nathan, and then Simeon. When Nathan was three, we began to notice some developmental lag. He didn't talk. He struggled learning to walk. My wife, who is a teacher, thought we should have him tested. We took him to a special program at the University of Illinois, and discovered that Nathan had several learning difficulties and would probably never function in a traditional classroom structure. Our shock and disappointment soon turned to resolve, and we were determined to help Nathan be all God had created him to be. Nothing more. Nothing less.

Learning most things was a challenge for Nate, but he seemed to enjoy life. Marcus, his older brother, helped Nathan learn to tie his shoes, put on his coat, and generally filled the usual role of older brother. Simeon, our youngest son, was the baby and worked that turf for all it was worth.

As Nathan grew, his kind, gentle, gregarious spirit infected our entire family. Our three boys seemed to enjoy each other's company, and fights were infrequent.

The year Nathan entered third grade, he learned something important about life. I was helping my wife with some household chores one day when I heard a commotion. My boys, all three of them, were on the verge of a full-blown fight in the backyard. I walked down the steps and into the midst of what looked like a Sumo wrestling match, with Nathan on one side and Simeon and Marcus on the other.

Using my *don't-even-think-about-not-doing-what-I'm-telling-you-to-do* voice, I pointed toward the back door and said, "Inside!"

All three boys sat on the floor in a semicircle, and I joined them. Their faces were red and sweaty, and their bodies convulsed with each breath. Silence is always an ally in these moments, so I just sat and looked at them for several seconds.

"What is going on?" I asked. "For the last few days, you guys have been at each other's throats, snipping and quarreling, and I want to know what's going on."

Marcus—a sixth-grader at the time, and the

leader — spoke first. "Dad, it's Nate. I don't know what's wrong with him, but for the last week, every time I say or do anything, he jumps on me."

Simeon raised one of his first grade hands, as though he were waiting for his teacher to call on him, while he pointed at Nathan with the other.

"That's right, Dad. It's not us. It's Nate."

I looked at Nathan, who sat slightly apart from the other two. Stone-like and stoic. Folded arms. Red face. A cauldron of indignation and anger.

"Nathan," I said, "What's going on?"

The statue broke its pose, as Nathan shrugged his shoulders.

"Nathan, I want an answer, and I want it *now.*"

Nathan's eyes hollowed, like twin caves gaping open and fixed, without any apparent focus. In quiet, almost monotone song, he began to describe the scene he was obviously watching on the projector of his memory.

"I go to special reading class every day. (Pause) And every day, there is this boy. He is a fourth-grader. He wait for me outside my room, and he walk alongside me. (Pause) He make fun of me, and he laugh at my reading book. (Pause) And he tell everyone in the play yard that I am dumb. (Pause) And he make me feel really bad in my heart."

Caves are wet, lonely, dark places, and these

two dripped slow, silent tears because of the sadness and pain they watched on memory's screen. And the room became acquainted with the sound of compassion; gentle, warm drops from father and brothers fell into now loyal laps.

Through my own tears, I looked at three sons who sat Indian-style on the floor of the family room. One of them felt alone. Two of them felt ashamed. All three of them waited for me to say something fatherly. I've never been comfortable speaking with lumps in my throat, so I decided to use my *the-man-who-controls-his-tongue-is-the-perfect-man voice* . . . and say nothing. I waited and I watched and I learned.

After many moments of silence, Marcus' wet face turned to Nathan's. He asked a simple question of his younger brother, but the implications of the asking were more than magical. They were profound. With quiet, almost awful resolve in his voice, he erased all of Nathan's aloneness. I watched Nathan's countenance change, as his older brother walked into the midst of the project room of his mind and stopped the film—with three words.

"Who's the guy?"

I suppose Marcus could have mapped out a strategy for what to say the next time the problem came up. He could have suggested that Nathan go to the principal. He could have said it didn't matter what people think. But the truth is, he chose to identify with Nathan by becoming personally involved and addressing the issue of might and authority and power. And for the next several weeks, when it was time to walk to special reading class, Marcus and Nathan walked together. Sixth-graders are a lot bigger than fourth-graders. The play yard looks different when you know a sixth-grader. The walk to special reading class takes on new dimensions when your big brother benevolently watches out for you.

If you see me on the street today, and I seem to be pushing and shoving, locked in a Sumo wrestling match with the rest of the world—angry for no apparent reason—it might be because there is a fourth-grader in my life who waits for me every day outside my door. His name may be Insecurity. It may be Obesity. It may be Loneliness. It may be Rejection. But every day, he is there. And every day, as I try to live my life, he comes alongside me, scoffing and laughing at my failures. He taunts and teases and tells me that I am dumb. And I feel really bad in my heart.

If you see me on the street today, remind me, will you? I need to hear it again. I have an Older Brother. He knows exactly how I feel. Death waited outside His classroom door and dragged

Him into another dark, wet cave, jeering—laughing because He dared assume that He was God. Meek, humble, dying Prince of Peace who stopped the projection screens with three small words: "It is finished!"

I've heard it all before, but I still need to be reminded. For three days, my Older Brother listened to all the taunts and jeers of hell. He looked Loneliness and Rejection in the face. He grabbed Grave by the throat, and choked eternal life out of Death. Then He turned on the Light of the world in that dark cave once and for all, and walked out. He sat down at God's right hand to watch the play yard. And in a graffiti-like scrawl, the Savior of the world wrote His own unique message in blood across the walls and stumbling blocks of life:

"In the world, you will have tribulation;
but be of good cheer, for I have
overcome the world!"

Jesus

AN ORDINARY DAY

THE SUN SHONE in the morning sky as she made her way to church. People drove up the winding road, found their parking places, and hurriedly made their way into the worship service. Fellowship on the church patio was warm and friendly as members chatted about the week just passed and the one about to start.

She had prepared well for this morning's challenge — a class of seven-year-olds. Lesson material in hand, she briskly walked up the steps and into her classroom. She was not alone. Her own young daughter accompanied her and would be one of her students. She waited several minutes to start class, knowing that people often find it difficult to make it on time to the 8 o'clock education hour. But no one came. No one that is, except her own daughter. Undaunted by the size of her class, she began to teach a roomful of empty chairs and her own child. She told the story of Jesus and how much He loves children. In eloquent simplicity, she talked of sin and forgiveness and eternal life — all in words a young child could understand. She shared about how much Jesus longs to live in the hearts of everyone who will let Him in. And then, lovingly, carefully, she asked that solitary student — her own daughter — if she would like to receive Jesus into her life.

If you had been passing by that ordinary classroom on that ordinary Sunday, you might have felt sorry for a teacher who had only one student. You might have felt a tinge of embarrassment for that student who had to sit with the teacher all by herself. But if you could have been a fly on the wall and listened as a young citizen was added to the kingdom of God, you would have known how important every single person is to Jesus. And you would have been honored to share in one of the most precious moments any parent can have, leading their own child into a personal relationship with Christ.

When you serve an extraordinary God, there is no such thing as an ordinary day. Ask Saul as he made his way toward Damascus. Ask the woman at the well, after she met a Man who told her everything she had done. Or better yet, ask that mother, that teacher, that lover of children, who taught one student and a roomful of empty chairs.

"I AIN'T TOO PURTY, BUT I'M CLEAN"

MA JONES WAS ninety-one. She was my great-grandmother, and her real name was Sarah, but everyone in the family called her "Ma." She lived virtually every day of her life less than twenty miles from where she was born, deep in the Ozark hills. My roots have been stained by that same red Missouri clay, and when I became engaged to a California girl, I wanted to introduce my wife-to-be to the matriarch of my family.

Randee and I drove the nearly 200 miles from St. Louis into the heart of Missouri's Ozark mountains. Ma's house was back off the main road across a ten-acre field. We could see her small frame scurrying around the garden that was planted every summer in front of her house. As we drove across the field, it was obvious that Ma knew company was coming, and she quickly began making her way out of the garden and around the side of the house.

The hot June sun made us grateful for air conditioning in the car, and as we got out, humidity slapped our faces with a vengeance. I could see Ma looking through the window, trying to persuade her ninety-one year old eyes to identify these two who were walking across her yard. It had been two years since I had been to Ma's house, so I knew she wouldn't be expecting me.

The old porch creaked a song of welcome as we made our way up the steps. The screen door opened before we could reach for it. Ma had recognized me, and her reaction was predictable. Without ceremony, she grabbed my neck, jerked me down to her level, and kissed the side of my face. Her voice had the texture of burlap with an Ozark drawl.

"Honey, it's been so long. I'm sure glad to see ya. Come on in and sit down." Ma's house smelled of old, antique tradition, and as we sat down together, she fumbled for the bow to her gingham bonnet.

"Those blamed hogs got in the garden this mornin', and I was after 'em with a hoe han'le!" It was obvious by the twinkle in her eye that the hogs were gone.

Her small frame lost its definition in the yards of material in her floppy dress. Ma was hard of hearing, but I was intent on being heard, so I leaned over and spoke in a louder-than-normal tone.

"Ma, I'm gonna get married next summer, and I wanted you to meet my financée. This is Randee. I met her in California where I go to college. She lives out there, and she flew back here to meet everybody."

Ma rose to her feet with a wrinkled dignity and walked across the room for a better look. Her dim eyes needed all the extra help they could get, and she brought her face within several inches of the girl I would one day marry. It was obvious she was pleased. Her pixie-like, toothless grin was a dead giveaway when Ma was tickled.

"I'm awful proud to meet you, honey," Ma said as she held out her bony, time-worn hand. Then, almost without missing a beat, she turned to me.

"She's awful purty, ain't she?"

The question required no answer. Ma often asked questions without really needing an answer. She'd already figured out the answer. All she wanted from me was a nod.

"I think so. I think she's real purty," I said, not really knowing why my speech had taken on hill-billy affectations.

Ma turned and walked back to what was obviously "her chair" by the way it conformed to the contours of her small frame. Her round, wire-rimmed glasses reflected the light from a nearby window, and I could see Missouri's blue sky in her eyes. She looked at Randee full in the face and introduced herself with one of the most confident displays of healthy self-image I have ever heard.

She said, "I ain't too purty, honey. But I'm clean."

No pretense. No offense. No guile. Just transparent humanity. I listened for the next hour or so to a ninety-one-year-old grandmother playing *Show and Tell* with the love of my life. Not *impressing.* Not *depressing.* Just disclosing. Incredible.

I am reminded of another story of transparency and love and bride and Groom.

The sun shone hot and the river flowed peacefully down the Galilean hillsides. John, the one they called the Baptist preached the fire of hell at one particular bend in the river, and his congregation listened intently. At the end of the sermon, a line formed, as it always did. People asked him to baptize them, as they always did. He preached so loud and long that it wasn't unusual for folks to finally get the message to "Repent!" and make their way down to be baptized.

But God happened to be in the neighborhood that day. He took the opportunity to introduce His

Son to the world. The Bridegroom and the bride, He thought, needed a proper prenuptial introduction. And so it was that the Son of God was introduced to the family of man.

Like all proud fathers, God wanted the best for His Child. He only had one Son, and He decided to make this most important introduction Himself. He stopped the procession of people walking into the river and had the Bridegroom walk to the front of the line and stand next to His best man, the Baptist. Then God looked full in the face of the bride-to-be and said to her, "This is My Son, whom I love; with Him I am well pleased."

I can almost picture those who were standing around watching the story unfold. The dove that came out of heaven was a nice touch, but the plain vanilla-looking Guy standing in the middle of the river with the Baptist certainly didn't look like the Son of God to any of them. Shouldn't He have a crown? Shouldn't He have royal robes? This Guy was too plain, too nondescript. He might be a Shepherd or a Carpenter or a Servant, but He couldn't possibly be a Savior, because everybody knows that Messiahs are handsome, well-dressed, royalty.

They missed the whole point. *We* missed the whole point. God never promised the world a handsome prince. The old prophet described

God's Son by saying, "He had no beauty or majesty to attract us to Him, nothing in His appearance that we should desire Him" (Isaiah 53:2). Ma Jones would have said, "He ain't too purty, but He's clean!"

Human beings are some of the most insecure people I've ever met. God gave us ears, but we don't hear. God gave us eyes, but we don't see. The only way He could ever get through to us was to send Total Transparency into the midst of our profound pretension. With sandal-footed humility, the Bridegroom walked out into the middle of the river of humanity and unashamedly spoke to the whole world.

No pretense. No offense. No guile. Perfect Deity housed in consummate humanity. Paradox of heaven with a wedding proposal in His hand:

"Here I am! I stand at the door and knock."

Revelation 3:20

THE WALK

THE KNOCK AT the door didn't seem unusual. It was the night before Thanksgiving, and the mob of family members we had invited for the holidays had already started arriving. But when I opened the door, I was surprised to find not a family member, but a policeman, with a pen and a pad of paper in his hand.

"Sorry to bother you tonight, sir," he said. "But the family across the street had a bicycle stolen from their yard this evening. They believe the time of the theft was between 4:30 and 5:45. I'm just checking with the neighbors to see if any of them saw anything unusual during that time period."

I knew it. I knew it! Why hadn't I acted on what I sensed?

I said, "Yes, I did see something unusual, and I can tell you when the bike was stolen. It was exactly 4:45."

The policeman's pen scribbled into action as he

began to write down my story.

Walking is one of my favorite things to do, and Fred is one of my favorite people. He's our family dog. He's not much on conversation, but he's great company. And he likes me. Fred and I had decided to take a walk, and I opened the garage door, snapped his green leash on his collar, and together we walked down our drive and turned left. Fred knew the way. We walked this direction quite a bit, and his small, apricot-colored body bounced as we started our course. I left the garage door open.

As we began, I noticed someone coming toward us about a block ahead. He was on the same side of the street as we were. About my size, height, and weight. As we got closer, I noticed how slowly he walked.

When Fred and I set out on our regular route, we *walk*. We don't lollygag along. We enjoy the sights and smells of our neighborhood, and we think to ourselves. *Mrs. Hampton is having pork chops tonight for dinner, I smell. Don's painting his garage door, I see.* That's the kind of thing we think of as we take our walk. But we walk briskly. We're not exploring. We're exercising. And to exercise, you have to keep up the pace.

The man who approached did not appear to have a destination. He wasn't into a cardiovascular workout. He sauntered; he ambled, aimlessly. His eyes looked over each house he passed. Round face; curly black hair; blue jacket and dark blue cotton pants. That's what he wore. And black, leather tennis shoes. I especially remembered his black tennis shoes.

As Fred and I came within a hundred feet or so of the man, he crossed the street. His hands were in his pockets, his eyes looked down at the ground and his feet never quickened their pace. It was as if he wanted to be invisible. He wanted to blend in to the scenery; become a part of the neighborhood. He did not want to seem exceptional or extraordinary. If his attitude had had a color, it would have been beige.

That guy's lookin' for somethin' to steal, Fred, I thought to myself.

I remembered my open garage door. I thought about my golf clubs, sitting right in front, near the door. My garage looks like a "garage sale in progress" most of the time, with golf clubs, and bicycles, and power tools in various stages of chaos and disorganization. It would be easy pickin's for someone who wanted to come by and help themselves.

But because this guy had crossed the street and was walking on the opposite side of the street from my house, I let the thought pass. As Fred and I walked away from the man and continued our jaunt down the street, I turned twice to see what he was doing. I looked around on two separate occasions to make sure he was still on the other side of the street from my house because I was worried about my golf clubs and my bicycles and my power tools.

I looked down at my watch, and it was 4:45. Not quite dark, light enough to see, but dusky dark.

The officer finished his note-taking and then look up at me. "Boy, I wish you had given us a call so we could have checked this guy out," he said.

My answer seemed logical.

"Well, you know how it is. You don't want to call the police to report a guy walking down the street. He wasn't doing anything wrong."

"Sure," he said. "I understand. But in a small community like this, if people don't seem to fit — if they seem foreign to the neighborhood — they probably are, and need to be reported so we can just make sure they're not trying to rip somebody off."

He thanked me and moved off into the darkness to talk to another neighbor, I suppose. But as I closed my front door, I thought about the little boy across the street. His bike was ripped-off by some turkey the day before Thanksgiving. A thief walked the streets of my neighborhood, and I didn't say a word.

There is, of course, another thief. This evil one, whose name is not worthy of capitalization, walks by my house and yours, today and every day. He is wormwood. He is beelzebub. He is lucifer, the author of all that is evil and foul and dank. His feet are shod with darkness, and his gaze upon the earth is continually evil, day and night. His methods for theft are subtle, insipid, barely detectable to all but the most sensitive of alarms. His thievery goes far beyond bicycles or power tools or golf clubs.

I didn't *see* him this morning, but he walked by my house. He was not in a hurry. He never is. He walked slowly, determined to steal anything he could lay his evil hands on. This thief noticed my unbridled joy, and my peace about the future, as he walked by. He salivated when he observed my tendency for leaving my thought life unattended. He peeked into the window of my life, and saw every area that was unsecured.

You may not have noticed him this morning, but this sinister adversary walked by your house too. And, as he walked by, he thought to himself, *As soon as he isn't looking . . . as soon as she turns her head . . . I will steal that joy. I will rob them of their peace. I will pillage and plunder and pilfer all they have left exposed to me.*

He is wrong. He is mistaken, for he is the one

who has been exposed. The Authority of Heaven stands watch. He who was and is and is to come stands as the Guardian, the Protector. The Advocate of Heaven has defeated the adversary of hell. The Author and Finisher of our faith neither slumbers nor sleeps, but takes His rightful place at the doorpost of our lives. He walks the streets of the neighborhood of His kingdom, Sentinel who exposes the thief for who he is—a liar and robber and a despiser of all that is good.

> "Your enemy the devil prowls
> around like a roaring lion."
>
> **1 Peter 5:8**

OUTSIDE

I SPEND SO MUCH of my time with safe, predictable, loving people. They call me "Pastor" and
they respect my office. The prestige of being a
pastor is something ministers enjoy, I think. But
when you walk away from the church office into a
world that has no idea who you are, you see a
totally different side of life.

I walked outside today. A television script writing seminar was being offered in San Francisco,
and I decided to attend.

I don't mind meetings where everyone wears a
name tag. In fact, I enjoy being able to call people
by their first names, even when we've just met. But
before things got too far along in the seminar, we
not only had to wear a name tag, we had to stand
and briefly introduce ourselves; where we worked,
why we were there, and what we hoped to get out
of the seminar. I enjoy being an anonymous pastor
once in a while, but I stood and gave my name and

position. I was the only pastor in the room. The mix of people attending the seminar fascinated me.

I was enjoying being with these people. They weren't stuffy people. They weren't plastic people. They weren't safe or churchy. They didn't pray before they started their meeting like I usually do. They weren't predictable. They were fresh and different . . . and lost. They were outside.

I heard a lot of things while I was outside today. A young Caucasian graduate student from Stanford sat behind me. He heard my introduction to the group, and later, during our coffee break, he came up to me and started a conversation. He said he was *interested in religious issues.* "I go to a church in Chinatown in San Francisco," he said. "I am very much interested in incorporating Eastern religious thought with Christianity. I find some of the ideas are very similar. I've been on a sort of spiritual journey for the truth in recent months, and I think I'm getting closer." He travels to China four times a year—hoping to find the truth, I suppose.

Before I could say anything to him, our break was over and we were called back to our places by the seminar leader. I invited the young man to lunch so we could talk more about his ideas. But he had a previous appointment with a friend and couldn't make it.

At lunchtime, when he left the room to meet his friend, I felt like I was watching him leave on a train. Not being able to talk with him about Christ was like running alongside a train, trying to talk to one of the passengers through a closed window. It was as though the train was picking up speed — faster and faster. Inside, it felt as if my spirit was standing by helplessly unable to catch up to the train of his life. My pastor-heart was frustrated as I watched a young man with so much to offer, search for answers in the wrong places. I could only wave as the train of his life continued down the track . . . I was outside.

I *did* have lunch with the publisher of a billiard magazine. He was a very mysterious man who told me he was working on a new method for teaching people how to play billiards. "It will transform the industry," he said. He came to this seminar to learn more about making a teaching video to market his idea. He looked over his shoulder and leaned toward me when he talked, as if he were afraid of being overheard. I confess my interest in billiards is only slightly greater than my interest in how to grow hydroponic tomatoes, but I tried to seem interested and cordial.

When the man finally remembered that I was the pastor, however, his demeanor changed. He lost his friendliness and seemed somewhat combative as he posed a trick question to me.

"I've asked this question to a lot of ministers, but no one has ever given me a good answer. Maybe you can." The condescendence in his voice convinced me of his insincere motive. "If God is good, and man is essentially bad, then why do so many people use the expression, 'By God, I've been had.' " I sensed he was searching my face for shock at hearing God's name used in such an unbecoming way.

He didn't want an answer. He wanted an argument. He wanted some esoteric nonsense. He wanted to hear me philosophize and sermonize and agonize over a silly question. Since I was convinced he didn't want an answer, I decided not to give him one. Instead, I looked as uninterested as I could. Not cold, mind you. Just disinterested, as if we were discussing hydroponic tomatoes and how they grow.

I said, "I'll answer your question if you can explain why the answer is essential to your relationship with God. . . . Pass the salt, please."

I looked away, munching on celery sticks. He stumbled over his lips as he tried to change the subject to something more benign. "So," he said after many silent seconds, "do you play much billiards?" No doubt about it. I was outside.

Later in the day, I talked to a young woman.

Her fashion told me she was outside too—navy blue suit with red trim and an "S" for Salvation, as in Salvation Army. Young and pretty and bright, she was.

She sought me out during an afternoon break. She said she'd just changed jobs with the Salvation Army. She left fifty kids on the streets of San Francisco in a youth ministry and took a job at the downtown Army headquarters in an administrative position. She said she didn't like it, even though it had only been a few weeks.

"I miss the kids. I was so involved in their lives. Now all I do is answer memos and telephones. Do you think I did the right thing?" she said.

I thought for a moment before I answered. Then, I put on my pastor's face. I used my pastor's voice. I gave a pastor's answer. I told her she must have the gift of administration, or they wouldn't have recognized her administrative abilities. I told her that God can use us anywhere, and that sometimes it takes time to see all that He is doing. I told her that God can use administrative gifts to accomplish His plans, and that He will send someone else to the streets and the fifty kids to be involved in their lives, if this is His will for her.

That was this morning, while I was outside.

But it's evening, now, and as I sit and listen to the sounds the night makes as it sleeps, I wonder.

I wonder if I could have said more to the young man who searched for *truth?* I wonder if I should have said more to a billiard magazine publisher who didn't care about the *truth?* I wonder if I said the right thing to the young woman who already knew the *truth,* but wasn't certain how the *truth* should be expressed through her life? I wonder how I did today, while I was outside?

Tomorrow, I go back inside—to my profession. Professional pastor. Professional administrator. Professional pray-er and talker. Tomorrow, I will be inside, in an office with a sign on the door that says, "Pastor." The first thing I'm going to do when I get to my office is open the window. I'm going to listen for the sounds of people looking for truth, and denying the truth, and dying without the truth. If the walls of my office are so insulated that those sounds can't disturb me. . . . If I can't hear those fifty kids on the streets of San Francisco as they play and laugh and search for the truth, then I'm pickin' up my desk and movin' it outside.

SCANNING THE HORIZON

THEY TRIED THEIR best to be good parents. Parenting any child is a terrific responsibility, but parenting this Child was truly an exceptional responsibility for Mary and Joseph. They had done everything the Law required, taking the Child to the temple in Jerusalem for dedication. They lived a quiet, unassuming life in the little hamlet of Nazareth with their Child, the Son of God.

Every year, they made the trek. Every year, they traveled the miles from Nazareth to Jerusalem for the Feast of the Passover. They planned carefully all year for the trip, but in their Son's twelfth year, they evidently didn't plan carefully enough.

They went to the Feast celebration just like they had done in previous years. But their Son was older now, and He probably liked to visit with other relatives and friends who were traveling to Jerusalem for Passover as well. There were, no doubt, many people on the road. It was probably not uncommon for the Boy Jesus to be away from Mary and Joseph for hours at a time during the journey.

As far as we know, the trip to Jerusalem was uneventful for the couple and their Son. They probably participated in the festivities like good Jewish believers. When the Feast was over, they left town — at least Joseph and Mary left town. Evidently, they thought Jesus was with them. They thought He was "in their company" (see Luke 2:44). When they did not see Him all day long, however, they became concerned. They went to family members. No one had seen Jesus. There was only one thing to do, now. They must return to Jerusalem to see if they could find Him.

As they began walking back to Jerusalem looking for their Son, they must have imagined that every figure they saw walking toward them in the distance was their Child. "Here comes someone approaching. Is that Him?" Mary might have said. "No. That boy is smaller than our Jesus and has longer hair," Joseph might have said. What were they thinking? What was *Joseph* thinking as he searched the horizon, hoping to see his Son walking toward them?

The streets of Jerusalem must have seemed less festive than a few days earlier, during the Feast — more frightening and lonely as they worried about their lost Boy. Three days Joseph and Mary searched the city looking for a twelve-year-old.

What was going through their minds? Surely they realized. Surely they understood their unique responsibility. God could have chosen any two people in the world in which to entrust His Son, but He had chosen the kind carpenter and the humble maiden.

Yes, they had done everything they knew to raise the Boy in the proper manner. But evidently, that wasn't enough. For now, in spite of their care and attention, Mary and Joseph had actually misplaced, lost, couldn't find, the one and only Son of God.

Of course, they ultimately did find Jesus. Remember? He was in the temple listening to the teachers; asking them questions. Mary chided Him for treating them so casually; for not telling them where He was. She said to Jesus, "Your father and I have been anxiously searching for You." Mary talked about the *worry* of a father, while Jesus talked about the *work* of the Father.

I'm so glad God put that story in the Bible. It helps me have perspective. You and I are responsible to care for and plan for and provide for our children every day. God could have sent them to any home He chose, but in His own time, He entrusted them to us. There will be those moments in the life of any parent, when it seems that the child God gave us cannot be found. Anxiety and worry becomes a heavy load to shoulder.

They may be runaways; they may be prodigals. They may be rebellious and disobedient and angry. They may not be out of our sight, yet we can't seem to find them. They may be sleeping in their bed at night and sitting at the kitchen table. They may be going to school every day, but they are still somehow not to be found. The lights are on, but nobody's home.

If you are searching for a son or daughter, and you scan the horizons of tomorrow wondering about their safety, praying for their welfare, keep it up. Pray every day. Pray all night, when you feel the need to. But be encouraged that the love of any father is nothing compared to the love of *the* Father. He is watching. He is reaching. He is searching, and He loves them more than you do.

TWO OLD MEN...
AND THEIR SONGS

THIS IS A STORY about two old men. They did not live in the same time or the same place, but they were both singers ... old singers who could *not* sing.

Charlie Clark's seat in church was toward the back, on the left. He did not enter God's house hastily. He walked slowly, deliberately. He carried a well worn Bible under his arm, and you could tell by the way he cradled it that the old Bible and the old man were good friends all week long. It seemed that Charlie started the church service before he ever sat down in the sanctuary. His manner and spirit reflected an attitude of reverence and preparedness for worship as he entered. Charlie's thinning white hair was always clean, and combed. He wore a coat and tie, well-matched and appropriate for a man of his age. As a former pastor, Charlie loved worship and the study of God's Word. Every Sunday, he and his wife took their customary place for morning worship.

On several occasions, I noticed that during the congregational singing, Charlie didn't sing. He always stood when the worship leader directed the congregation to do so. He always held a hymnal in his hand and seemed to be following along with his eyes as the hymns were being sung. But Charlie Clark rarely opened his mouth. He almost *never* sang a note in church.

It seemed strange to me that such a devout man of God would not enter into the singing. It was obvious by his manner and life that he loved God very much. His attendance at virtually every worship service underscored his devotion to God's house. But he never sang.

As a young pastor, I often greeted members and friends as they left the sanctuary on Sunday mornings. Charlie's custom was to tell me he loved me — every Sunday. I looked forward to seeing Charlie and his wife, because when I saw them coming up the aisle toward the back of the church, I knew what Charlie would say. With the glint and twinkle of genuine Christian love in his eyes, the old man would gently reach for my hand, put his other arm around my shoulder, and say, "I just want you to know I love you, Buddy."

And I loved the old man. Maybe that is why I spoke to him on one particular Sunday as he left the sanctuary about why he did not sing during the congregational worship time.

"Charlie," I said, "I have noticed that you don't sing the hymns during the congregational singing. Why is that?"

Charlie's gentle manner made me feel like I could ask him anything. His warmth invited me. His smile asked me into his life, and we sat down together on a pew toward the back of the church. He wanted to explain something to me, he said.

"Doc, I need to tell you something. When I don't sing, it's not because I don't feel the song. I just don't want to bother anyone around me. I can't sing. I've heard you say we all need to lift our voices in song. But you've never heard me sing. If I did, I'd distract everyone around me and get them off the note. I can't sing. So I just follow the words in my mind."

It is difficult for me to imagine life without singing. I hear music in the midst of the loudest chaos. Music is like a very best friend for me. When Charlie sat next to me on the back pew of the church gently holding my arm and telling me he couldn't sing, I remember thinking how terribly lonely life would be without a song. I wanted to give my old friend a song.

"Charlie," I said, "Who told you couldn't sing?"

"Everybody knows I can't sing, Pastor. I hear

the melody as it goes by, but I can't make my voice get on board. I'm a monotone. It's awful when I try to sing."

I put my arm around the old man, and I looked into his saintly face. He was an elder to me in every sense of that biblical term, and I revered him. I loved him. Now, my pastor heart wanted to teach him, to encourage him, to free the song of his life.

"Charlie," I began, "the voice you have is from God. It was factory-installed. I understand that you may be a monotone. But Charlie, even a stopped clock is right twice a day. Sing your note, Charlie. Sing it loudly. Sing it as unto the Lord. Sooner or later, the melody of the song will cross your note, and when it does, you're going to be right on key. You may have to wait the whole song until your note comes by, but sooner or later, it *will* and you'll be right on! And when you sing that note, Charlie, all heaven will stop to listen. I believe the angels will stop what they're doing, and say, 'Shh. Be quiet. Charlie's about to sing his song.' " Charlie hugged my neck and said, "OK, Pastor. I'll try."

After our lesson on singing, I began noticing that Charlie opened his mouth when he sang in church. He seemed to be making his joyful noise unto the Lord. He turned in the hymnal to the song we were to sing and seemed to enjoy entering into the song service.

My eyes would occasionally meet his as I led the congregation in a great hymn. It was easy to see when we were on Charlie's note. I knew the minute the wind of melody had passed his way. It was as if he were soaring into the heavens on its updraft. His head would tilt back. His eyes would lift up. We were there, all right. It was time. Charlie's note was here, and he sang it so all heaven could hear. *Sing, Charlie! Sing for all you're worth,* I would think to myself.

Charlie sings in heaven now. But the picture of my old friend singing in church is tucked away safely in my memory, and I enjoy remembering the wonderful way he worshiped.

Maybe that is why I like the story of the second old man so much. He must have had white hair like Charlie's. He was old, and spent a lot of time in God's house. And he waited to sing his song until it was time.

He waited every day. His dim eyes had seen much in life, but they hadn't seen it all. Not yet. So he waited. He was a righteous man, a devout man, who loved God and His house. No one probably paid much attention to the old man, as he sat every day in the temple courts. There were a lot of old men scattered throughout the temple court area.

The Bible doesn't say it, but I think he hummed as he sat there.

That's right. I think he hummed a melody as he sat there day after day. I think he hummed softly, because he didn't sing that well. At times, he may have hummed to himself, so he wouldn't bother the people who passed by. I'm not positive, mind you, but I believe he hummed a song and waited.

He wasn't worried about dying. He hadn't seen *everything* yet, and God had already told him that he wouldn't die until his eyes had seen the Light.

The morning of his premier performance probably started like every other morning. He got up, got dressed, and took care of a few things around the house before he walked to the temple courts to wait. But this morning was different. The Spirit drove him and moved him and urged him along. It was time. He mustn't miss his cue.

He took his seat in the temple courts. People hurried in and out—teachers of the Law, preoccupied with their own agendas, not noticing that the old man was about to sing. The drone of the temple court area must have sounded like an orchestra running before the concert begins. I can almost see the old man humming, vocalizing to himself in preparation for what was about to happen.

Can't you imagine the Maestro of heaven stepping to the podium, baton in hand, as the young couple with the Child walked across the stage of the temple courts. Then, the Maestro raised His hands as the couple handed the Child to the old man, and the Maestro nodded for him to begin the song.

Now, Simeon, now. Don't wait. Don't hold back. The melody of heaven has crossed your life. Sing, Simeon. Sing. All heaven and earth will listen. Lift up your head, throw the window of your soul open, and sing your song! Scribes are ready to record your lyric of praise. They will take down your every word. So, sing!

The old man didn't hum softly to himself. Instead, he sang an unashamed song, with head tilted back and eyes lifted to God. This was not a time for timorous note. Eternal proclamation demands a formidable song. His arms were filled with baby; his heart was filled with praise and adoration. He sang no mother's lullaby, did Simeon. He sang a complete oratorio in just four, short verses of Luke, chapter two:

> Sovereign Lord, as You have promised,
> You now dismiss Your servant in peace.
> For my eyes have seen Your salvation,
> which You have prepared
> in the sight of all people,
> a light for revelation to the Gentiles
> and for glory to Your people Israel.

What a song the old man sang. When he was through, I believe all heaven erupted in a thunderous ovation. The old man's song was worth the wait, and the magnificence of his music has inspired composers ever since.

Two old men, who didn't know they could sing. I love those two old men. I love to remember how they sang. I love one of them so much, my youngest son is named after him. *Simeon* means, "God heard."

Don't be mislead. God is listening. The Maestro stands on the podium every day—baton in hand, arms raised, ready to begin. He will direct you. He is leading you. His sense of timing and melody are wonderful. Sing the song of your life to Him, even if you think you only have one note. Others around you may be passing by. They may not seem to appreciate the song. Sing anyway.

Sing like Charlie, with head back, eyes up. Heaven is watching. Heaven listens, for even angels can't sing the song of the redeemed like us. They've never been lost. Sing like Simeon—patient, waiting for what God had said. Sing . . . let the concert begin . . . There's only one way to sing the song of songs. Sing it with all you've got!

PETER

IT'S ONLY 5:30 on Sunday morning, and I feel like I've already been to church—because of Peter.

I like to arrive on Sundays very early, to spend extra time in prayer and prepare for the busy day of ministry. It is my custom to stop at a convenience store near the church for a quick cup of coffee before driving on to the church campus. Peter works at that convenience store on weekends, and I always look forward to our brief encounter on Sunday mornings.

Peter is from Pakistan. He moved here a few years ago as a victim of religious persecution. You see, Pakistan is a Muslim country—very Muslim. And Peter is a Christian man—very Christian. The incompatibilities of his faith and those around him made his life very difficult, and he was finally forced to move here for the protection of his family. He and his wife and children have been attending our church for several months now.

By professional training, Peter is an accountant. But it was difficult for him to find a job as an accountant when he first arrived in the area. For many weeks, he was unemployed. Finally, after much searching and struggle, he got a job at the local convenience store working nights. Then, about two months ago, Peter landed a job with a local insurance firm. He decided to keep his night job on the weekends because he could use the extra cash. So, Peter works seven days a week. I suppose to be more accurate, he works five days a week, and then works all night Friday and all night Saturday.

So, when I see Peter early on Sunday mornings, he's been up nearly twenty-four hours. He gets off work at about 7 on Sunday mornings, but he doesn't go home. He goes to church. After being up all night, he sits through an education hour, where he is an active part of a Sunday School class, and then morning worship.

As I casually sipped my coffee, I leaned against the counter between us and asked Peter if he ever got sleepy during the sermon. "You know, if you planned it just right," I joked, "and sat behind a lady with a big hat on Sunday morning, you might be able to catch a few winks without the preacher knowing you're asleep."

He smiled, and said, "Oh, no, Pastor. I never sleep in church. There is too much to hear, and I need it all. I use everything that is said after I leave church to minister to people I meet through the week . . . like what happened this week."

A dear devotion to Christ crept into Peter's voice when he spoke, and I felt there might be more to his story if I took a moment to listen. And I took a moment and I listened, and indeed, there was more to his story.

"Two people this week, Pastor. Two people this week I led to the Lord, standing where you are standing now, across this counter. They are night people. They come into this store at 2, 3, 4 in the morning, and they are searching for something. I help them find it. They think they are searching for beer or a night club or some such thing. I know they are searching for Jesus, and I tell them about Him."

Peter was animated and alive as he talked now. The early morning weariness that should plague anyone who has been up all night was absent from Peter's countenance. He talked with his hands. He talked with his face, expressions of excitement, awake and alert.

"One came in last Friday night," he continued. "He was a German man. He came in wanting some beer about 2 in the morning. We were all alone in the store, and I told him about Christ. For one-and-a-half hours, Pastor, I shared my faith with him. I told him about the church and about my Jesus."

When Peter talked of "my Jesus," a personal identification and ownership of grace seemed to splash all over his words. He was under orders; a man on a mission, who knew the Commander-in-Chief as a Brother and Friend and Confidant. I love to hear people who have been touched by God tell the story of how they touch others with Him. And Peter was in rare form as he continued the story.

"I prayed with the man, Pastor, and he accepted the Lord standing right where you are standing. He came through these doors loud and laughing and empty in his life. When he walked out the door, he was quiet and changed. There was real peace on his face."

What about the other person Peter had mentioned, I wondered. "Tell me about the other person, Peter."

He needed little encouragement now, as he stood next to the cash register, holding the money for my coffee in his hand.

"The other man came in about midnight this last evening. He was a black man who came into the store and asked me for directions to a night club. I asked him, 'Why are you looking for a night club?' He said he wanted to go there for fun. I told him if he was looking for real fulfillment and joy, I could help him find it. We were all alone in the store, Pastor. It was as if the Lord kept customers away so we could talk about Jesus. I led the man to the Lord at about 1 this morning. I have invited him to join me in the services later today. He lives in Oakland, and I am hoping he will come."

Peter now looked down at the cash register, and punched in the price of my coffee. He had finished his story, and other customers were coming through the door. His last words to me as I walked out of the little convenience store with a cup of coffee in my hand were, "I'll see you later, Pastor, in church."

You've been in church, Peter. You are the church . . . the only church there is. You're what Jesus intended all along; a pile of dead, lifeless rocks that would spring to life when Resurrection rolled the stone away. You're what Jesus had in mind when He talked to another Peter; another rock. And now, living stones like you, Peter, make up a wonderful, eternal edifice called the church. And whether we are the church gathered on Sunday morning, or the church scattered at midnight on Friday night, we all need to stay awake.

71

Stay awake, Peter. And stay awake, church. There will be those migrants who are looking for direction and hope and life. Stay open to what God has set in motion in your life, and share it with those who happen your way. On Saturday night at 1 in the morning or Thursday afternoon at 4. If those two wanderers had knocked on the door of the building where we meet to worship, if they had made their way onto these grounds in the middle of the night, they would have found an empty hull, dark and void of life. Thank God, they found the church . . . His church . . . wide-awake at 1 in the morning. And we never close.

THE DRIVE

I'M DEFINITELY getting older. One of the ways I know that is by how long it takes me to recover from a particularly hard day. My day started before 6 this morning, and I finally locked the doors of the church about 9 o'clock. Weariness stood with me; lassitude turned the key. I was tired.

Simeon—fifteen-year-old, 175 pound, five-foot-eleven-inch baby of our family—had somehow missed the last bus for home earlier in the evening, and since his school was close to my office, he decided to wait with Dad and work on homework. He carried his book bag. And as the night cooled our faces, we walked together across the church parking lot toward the tan Chevy.

Simeon has a wonderful gift. He can fill even the most mundane moment with noise and talk and stories about the happenings of his day. He's the kind of guy who can see a movie and remember not only all the characters and the plot, but the dialogue. If you were to ask Simeon about a movie he had seen, he wouldn't give you a review, he'd give you a replay. And his countenance, his temperament, and his personage, all join in, as he tells and explains and finds significance in details others might not notice.

Well, tonight, as I walked across the church parking lot, I heard Simeon reconstruct his day. But the sound of his voice was something I had learned to tune out, like the music you hear while you're looking for a ripe tomato in a grocery store. It's there, but you pay little attention to it. And as we walked, the weariness of my day was speaking louder to me than the minutia of Simeon's day. I was already in my "unwind" mode and thinking about home and bed.

But as we approached the car, I did something out of total spontaneity that put the alleluia on a day that Simeon will never forget.

I took the keys to the tan Chevy out of my pocket, and instead of unlocking the doors of the car, I tossed them to Simeon.

"I'm awful tired tonight, Pal. Would you mind driving home?"

Driving home? Him? Simeon? This man-child who sat in an infant seat just yesterday (or was it the day before)? Simeon ... whose feet didn't touch the pedals of his bike when he was in the third grade? Simeon-the-Youngest? That Simeon?

There are some things a person is born with. One of them is the ability to catch the keys to the car when Dad tosses them. We *learn* how to ride a bike. We *learn* our multiplication tables. But catching the keys to the car in midair is not a learned behavior. Instinct took over for Simeon; his mouth dropped, and so did his book bag, as he caught the keys I tossed his way.

"Yeah ... sure Dad," he said.

Simeon's instant replay of his day stopped as he caught those keys, and I watched as he slammed the transmission of his mind into another gear. This would be his maiden voyage. *Nonchalant* is a terribly important look when you're a young man about to make your first test flight behind the wheel of a tan Chevy. And Simeon had that look. He unlocked the car door like any responsible driver would. He slid his fifteen-year-old frame into the driver's seat and leaned across to unlock the door on the passenger side. The fact that he had forgotten his book bag lying in the parking lot next to the car diminished only slightly his casual demeanor. I looked the other way as he got out of the car, picked up his books, and quickly tossed them in the back seat.

He buckled in (and so did I). He put the keys in the ignition and started the car. No one had to tell him that's what you do first. He had seen it done thousands of times. Even though my mind was tired, I was able to sense the profoundness of what this moment represented. I wanted to savor it, like a wonderfully rich dessert that you eat with a small fork, in tiny, deliberate bites.

Dark and quiet filled the car and I decided to break the silence with an expression of gratitude, hoping that small talk would ease the anxiety of my chauffeur.

"I sure apprecite this, Sim. There are some days when I just don't feel like drivin'."

"Oh, no problem, Dad. I don't mind at all."

As Simeon talked, his eyes scanned the dash for the gearshift indicator. Without any hesitation, he confidently pulled the lever down. He pulled with such confidence, in fact, that he passed the R for Reverse, and the N for Neutral and was well on his way toward passing the D for Drive before he realized that his first move needed to be backward, since our car was parked close to the building. Like a pro, he quickly adjusted the lever upward until the arrow pointed to R. With only a slight hesitation now, he took his foot off the brake pedal.

No doubt about it. Simeon was driving.

I gave none of the traditional father-to-son instructions to Simeon on this, his first session behind the wheel. It seemed to me that there would be other days and other times and other drives for talking about checking mirrors and turning on the directional signals and watching the speedometer. We were alone, my youngest son and me. As the youngest, Simeon often had to listen to a barrage of information and advice from his two older brothers. He rarely got to be the expert about any of the ordinary experiences of life, because both of them had preceded him. Older brothers are experts on almost everything, you know. But for tonight – in the church parking lot behind the wheel of that tan Chevy – Simeon was the master of his own destiny, and I determined not to rob him of the significance of this moment with demeaning advice about how to keep the car in the middle of the road.

The empty parking lot looked like a runway without lights, as we made our way to its edge, and then down the winding drive. Our adventure would be a short journey, much of it down an isolated frontage road. Simeon seemed to understand his own limitations and drove slowly, almost resolutely through the dark night toward home.

What this moment represented for me was an opportunity to experience my son growing up. In Illinois, where I come from, if you take an evening walk into a field of corn in mid-July after an all-day rain, you can actually hear the corn grow, if you listen carefully. You can hear the corn stalks pop and twist, reaching and stretching like a baby waking from a nap. Well, tonight, I listened to my son—my youngest son, who is fifteen. I listened to him drive the car. I listened to him breathe and sigh and relax and yes—grow. I watch him every day, and I listen to his stories. I notice that his shirts are bigger, and his voice is deeper. I'm not convinced I always see him grow. But tonight, on a safe, quiet stretch of lonely road, I watched him grow, as he sat in the driver's seat, and I was his first passenger. I had not realized that metamorphosis made such a loud noise. But from fifteen to "forever-changed" is a loud noise indeed.

No one else was around. We had a long stretch of isolated streets and roads ahead of us and *he* was in control. For this brief snapshot of time, the keys in the ignition were Simeon's keys. And the tan Chevy was not the family car, but Simeon's car. Dad sat next to him. In fact, this was Dad's idea, and the freedom and liberty of this moment was like wind blowing in his face.

He turned on the radio. He sat up tall and straight like a stalk of Illinois corn in mid-July. His back didn't touch the seat, and he leaned into the steering wheel as though the wind were filling his sails. He asked me three times in seven minutes, "How'm I doin', Dad?"

There's only one response to a question like that when you're growing corn in the flat prairies of Illinois—"Fine. You're doin' just fine."

Our driveway came too soon for Simeon, I suppose. But he slowed as we approached home and made an acceptable left turn into our drive. He turned off the key, looking proud to have safely navigated the seven-minute trip home. I tried not to notice that he hadn't put the car into *Park* before he turned off the engine. He couldn't get the key out of the ignition and had to restart the car and try again.

"No big deal," I said. "I do that all the time." That reassurance seemed to help his obvious embarrassment, and we got out and strolled into the house together.

I watched as Simeon held the keys in his hand as long as he thought he dare, before he put them on the key rack in the entry. His two older brothers watched sports scores on the news broadcast as Simeon walked tall, and straight, almost triumphantly, and took his seat as a young man among young men.

"I drove home tonight for Dad. He was too tired."

I could tell by Simeon's expression that he hoped for some response or acknowledgment. But older brothers learn to tune out younger ones, like people tune out the music that plays in a grocery store while you look for a ripe tomato. His brothers were too preoccupied with the baseball scores on the television to notice Simeon standing tall and grown. They probably never even think about their own first driving experience . . . way back then.

Their ignoring could not subdue his delight. Out of the corner of my eye, I watched Simeon's face. His eyes told me he was retracing our journey home from the church parking lot. He sat on our overstuffed couch, leaned back, folded his hands behind his head, and looked up to the ceiling. He wasn't interested in the sports on TV, or the Cardinals score, or the chocolate cake and milk Mom had waiting in the kitchen. The wings of this butterfly had dried enough to allow him to take his first flight, and he would never be content with a cocoon again.

How long? How long has it been since you felt Him toss you the keys and say, "Go for it. I'm the Dad. I'm sitting here right next to you, and I say it's OK. Turn on the key. Put it into gear. What do you say? Let's take a drive . . . forward!"

There may be something you'd like to do, but no one has given you the permission or encouragement or offered to go along with you on your first try. No one has stepped to the front of your life and said, "Go ahead."

The world says you're too young or too old or too inept. The world says you're just a learner; you have no experience, no license, no permission.

Well, that may be what the world says. But it isn't what God says.

God says, "I'm right here."

God says, "I will never leave you, or forsake you."

God sent a Counselor to instruct and teach and lead. He knows the way home. He knows about the drive. He sees tomorrow and yesterday, and they both look just alike to Him. He is the keeper of the keys, and He revels in the thought that you are growing.

You need no more permission than that. Go ahead. Grow for it.

"But the Counselor, the Holy spirit, whom the Father will send in My name, will teach you all things and will remind you of everything I have said to you."

Jesus

FINISHED WELL

HER NAME WAS Martha, and I preached her funeral last week. She was old and frail . . . and she finished well.

She taught the junior boys class when I was a kid, in the musty old basement of a little neighborhood church — every student a personal missionary project. I'm not sure Sunday School for junior boys was an idea God thought of, because of the way junior boys are put together. He created junior boys with wiggles, and whispers, and wonderings-out-loud about kites and frogs and fences that need to be climbed. It's difficult for a junior boy to hear what God has to say in a musty, old basement of a tiny church and a wrinkled grandma-type standing up front next to a flannelgraph.

She must have known that, because more often than not, she'd abandon that basement tomb and resurrect the junior boys in her class to the sunshine outside. We would take walks through the neighborhood (yes, during classtime on Sunday mornings!), looking for treasures and listening to the sounds of God's creation. She seemed to take particular delight in introducing boys, who wondered about everything, to a God who created every wonder.

We made slings and pretended we were David, slaying Goliath. (And I hit David Cook with one of my five, smooth stones. And we'd sit on a grassy knoll and lie on our backs looking up at the clouds and practice saying the Twenty-third Psalm. She could almost make me see the sheep on the Galilean hillside as those cumulus clouds rolled by.

When I was growing up, my family was convinced that the place to be on Sunday nights was in church. My young eyes were almost always sleepy before the preacher got started, and I would often slumber during the message. But I can still picture Martha, down at the altar at the close of the service. She always chose the same spot to pray, down on the left, in a corner by herself. She always took her Bible. And when she prayed, I was convinced God Himself was sitting in a chair, with rapt attention, listening to everything she had to say. It was at her side on one of those sleepy Sunday nights that I asked Jesus to be my Savior. He still is.

Years later, when she learned that I would be going away to school to study for the ministry, she called me to her humble little house for a farewell before I left.

"I want you to know that I will be praying for you every day," she said. "I will pray for your wisdom, not for your wealth or fame or anything else. If Solomon needed wisdom and prayed for it, it must be a good thing to have. And so, I will pray that God gives you much wisdom and insight in your future ministry."

During my time at school, I received many letters from Martha, encouraging me and telling me she was still praying for me and for wisdom.

When I learned that she was gravely ill and probably would not survive the week, I made arrangements to fly from California to Illinois to see her and say good-bye. She was hospitalized, and I made the drive from the airport to the hospital hoping she would still be there when I arrived.

I walked into the room and saw her frail frame lying in a bed that was designed for someone much bigger. Gray, thin hair pulled back into a tight bun, lovely pink gown, with baby-blue ribbon ties. Feeble face of weathered life. Lines etched in that face, lines drawn by the seasons—winters of mourning and summers of caring. She looked asleep, but a coma caused her quiet serenity. I could not help myself. I smiled. I stood, a grown man yet a boy next to her bed, and for many moments, I looked into her old, wrinkled face and I smiled. I smiled for two reasons.

I smiled when I saw her because I remembered her sense of humor and her faith and her person. The memory of her life was in full bloom in my mind, and I enjoyed and savored the aroma of her faith.

The second reason I smiled was because, as I stood there in her room, I sensed that Martha was only hours away from an event she had waited for and longed for all her life. She was almost there — almost finished — and she had lived and trusted and walked before God in faithfulness and excellence. A Scripture verse ran through my mind as I stood there looking into her godly face. It was delivered by another old war-horse of the faith, just before he left for Home:

"The time has come for my departure.
I have fought the good fight,
I have finished the race, I have kept the faith.
Now there is in store for me the crown of righteousness,
which the Lord, the righteous Judge,
will award to me on that day — and not only to me,
but also to all who have longed for His appearing."

2 Timothy 4:6-7

LATIN

WHEN I STARTED the ninth grade, my counselor said that I would need to take a foreign language because colleges required two years of a foreign language for admissions. Several languages were offered at my high school, but my counselor (who was very smart) suggested I take Latin. Her recommendation seemed to flow from two basic wells of thought.

"First," she said, "Latin is the mother of all languages. Many of our English words come from Latin derivatives, and if you have a good, solid base in Latin, you'll be better prepared for future study in English." Her statement made perfect sense to me. (Up to that point in time, I had given very little thought to where English came from, but I thought it might be nice to check it out.)

"Second," she continued, "I think you'll enjoy the intellectual challenge of the study." Now emotion in her voice caused the pitch to rise a bit, and she seemed to lose touch with reality for a moment, as she turned her back to me and stared out the window. She talked slowly, deliberately as one who was remembering a time long-since passed. "I studied Latin for four years and loved every moment of it. It's a beautiful language with much nuance and rich color."

I didn't know anything about *nuance,* but it sounded kind of French to me. My counselor made Latin sound so reasonable and challenging and . . . necessary. I signed on the dotted line. I enrolled. And so it was, that without fully knowing what I was getting into, I began a long night's journey down the Appian Way.

Mr. Drowbowski (not his real name) was my first Latin teacher. He could best be described as serious — about *everything.*

He was *serious* about his music. He said his favorite key was C sharp minor because he loved the morose feeling it produced. (He didn't say so, but I think he also read a lot of Edgar Allen Poe.) He was *serious* about the piano and hoped to be a concert pianist someday. He was *serious* about practice. He told us in class that he practiced piano eight hours on Saturdays and eight hours on Sundays.

But most of all, Mr. Drowbowski was *serious* — very serious — about "the mother of all languages."

"There are some general thoughts about the

language," he said, "which will be beneficial for your understanding." (Mr. Drowbowski always called Latin *the language,* reverently, with folded hands, using the same voice some people do when they talk about *the arts* or *the theatre.*)

"First of all, Latin is not a spoken language. It is a written language." His statement caused a wrinkle to appear on my forehead. Uneasiness entered my mind and began looking for a place to sit.

I wondered why, if Latin could be written, it couldn't be spoken. I didn't wonder out loud though. I somehow knew that my teacher wouldn't take kindly to questions like that, so I just wondered to myself. I couldn't accept what Mr. Drowbowski said in its entirety. What good was it to know a language you couldn't speak? I looked forward to proving him wrong. One of the reasons I signed up for a foreign language in the first place was so I could talk to my friends without anyone around knowing what I was saying. I sat up straighter than usual, not wanting to miss what Mr. Drowbowski would say next. He was beginning to make me nervous.

"In addition to our study of the language, we will be focusing on the culture and life of the Roman Empire. It was an incredible culture, rich in nuance and color." Mr. Drowbowski turned his back on the class and stared out the window, just like my counselor had done earlier. His voice had a far-off quality just like my counselor's voice. And he spoke of *nuance* and rich color, just like my counselor. But he convinced me his train of thought was on a different track than mine and going in the opposite direction. I still remember wishing I knew what *nuance* meant.

As my teacher continued to talk, two of my classmates walked down the aisles placing a text on each desk. I tuned Mr. Drowbowski out for a moment, opened my new Latin book, and began to thumb through its pages to see what was in store. Like most texts, there were lots of words and lots of exercises. But, in this text, on almost every page, there were pictures.

Some of the pictures were of ruins, broken-down buildings, and old roads with grass and weeds growing in the middle of them. One of the pictures had a caption about a place where Julius Caesar had won a famous battle. The book was filled with black-and-white photographs of statues in various stages of undress, which caused me to wonder about the propriety of *the mother of all languages.* This didn't look like nearly as much fun as my counselor had said it was.

Mr. Drowbowski droned on about conjugations, verb tenses, and vocabulary tests. I continued to flip through the text, noticing that togas had a remarkable resemblance to my bathrobe and that Roman sandals looked for all the world like thongs. Anxiety squeezed my throat, but not so tightly that I couldn't ask a questions.

"Excuse me, Mr. Drowbowski, but did I hear you say we will have a vocabulary test *every week?*" I said. His answer brought no comfort to my now Latin-troubled life.

"Yes," he said. "There will be a thorough vocabulary test every Friday."

I continued glancing through the book, hoping for a ray of light, all the while getting closer and closer to a full-blown clinical depression about two years of incarceration with mother Latin. My hopes raised a bit when I flipped past a cartoon in the text book. *Maybe there are some jokes in this book,* I thought.

The cartoon was a policeman who had obviously stopped a young motorist in a convertible and was writing out a traffic ticket. He stood next to the car, looking down on the young man who was driving. The caption of that cartoon is one of the few things I remember about Latin. *"Ubi est signis?"* — "Where's the fire?" Was that supposed to be funny? Was that a joke in Latin?

Obviously, the reality of *nuance* and rich color were staring me in the face. Uneasiness had found a place to sit now, and depression sprawled out on the floor of my life, like a visiting relative with a sleeping bag. My life made a slow, dirge-like pass before my eyes, and I put my face into my hands. This was going to be boring. It was *not* going to be fun.

Two years. I made it through Latin for two years. Straight D's. Not "Improving slightly." Not "Exemplary attitude." Not "A joy to have in class." For two years, the epitaph of my report card in Latin read, "Needs more work." I could feel Mr. Drowbowski as he walked by my desk at the end of every quarter. I could hear his music in C sharp minor as he dropped the dreaded notice on my desk. I felt guilty. I had betrayed the mother of all languages, and what good was I now? How could I have missed the *nuance* and rich color that my counselor and my teacher kept telling me were there? I know they were there. Debbie Spengler sat right in front of me for two years, and she made straight A's. She knew nuance. She reveled in every rich color. But me? All I could do was keep asking that question: "Where's the fire?" I truly felt like a failure.

I buried those feelings for a long time. Gradually, however, as I grew older, I began to develop a sense that there is a lot more to life than Latin. I did well in English and enjoyed writing. I earned a degree in music and even composed and published some of it.

But I never wrote anything in C sharp minor because I don't hear the song of life in C sharp minor. And I went on down the road of my life without looking back on the Appian Way or togas or statues without any arms. I didn't make a big deal of it, but I thanked God I didn't have to conjugate any more verbs when I got out of Latin.

Got anything like that in your life? You were told when you were younger that you had to read it or learn it or practice it because if you didn't, then (implied) something bad would happen to you.

Give yourself a break. Whatever it was, let it go. I'm convinced it's OK not to like the key of C sharp minor. It's OK not to think *Ubi est signis* is funny. God made us all unique, and He expected us to maintain that uniqueness in the midst of intellectual, spiritual, moral discipline. I may need to learn about togas, but I'll never enjoy wearing one. And thongs have always given me blisters between my toes.

"Brothers, I do not consider myself yet
to have taken hold of it. But one thing I do:
Forgetting what is behind and straining toward
what is ahead, I press on toward the goal to win
the prize for which God has called me heavenward
in Christ Jesus. All of us who are mature should
take such a view of things. And if on some point you
think differently, that too God will make clear to you."

Philippians 3:13-15

SUNRISE

I GET UP EARLY almost every morning to read and write and think. And this morning, as I was reading and writing and thinking, I glanced out the window, and I noticed it. In fact, it was such a profoundly beautiful noticing that I stopped what I was doing, put on my brown leather jacket, and walked outside of my office to appreciate it from a closer venue.

I stood on the walk of our church campus and looked out across the lawn. It's a beautiful view, high atop a hill, overlooking a wide valley below. I leaned against a post and tried to be as quiet as possible. No one else was around. I folded my arms and tilted my head and took a long, deep drink with my eyes.

It was time. The sun was coming up.

The television networks didn't televise it, but they should have. (They don't televise a lot of good things, you know.) In fact, as nearly as I could tell, I was the only one watching—live, and in color. The cars on the freeway below me drove right on by. They drove right past the morning waking up. And the people in those cars didn't seem to notice that night was calling it a day.

I wanted to point at the dawn, and I wanted to call to those people, "Hey! Turn around and look behind you. You're so busy driving west, toward work and money and bosses and stuff, that you're missing it. You're missing the show. You're missing the only morning this day will ever have."

I wanted to hold up a giant poster that read, "If you take the time to stop and look at what's behind you, you won't be disappointed. It's incredible!"

I wanted to wave my arms at all of them and say, "Why don't you glance in your mirror? It'll only take a second. It's worth the effort. The sun's coming up, and you haven't even noticed it."

That's what I wanted to say—but I didn't. I just stood there in my brown leather jacket, leaning against a post. For several moments I watched the palette of the morning sky change colors—each scene more beautiful than the last—each moment filled with its own glory and fragile splendor.

What I saw, and what you see as you read these words are very different. I saw colors—red mixed with orange and pink and a touch of gray.

You see words.

I saw hills, black as coal, standing in the distance. And those black hills wore a quilt of lights that blinked and winked and twinkled as darkness yielded to the dawn.

You see a description.

I saw the canvas on which this magnificence was painted; a sky spread from the southeast and wrapped toward the north horizon like a wide ribbon.

You see nouns and modifiers and verbs.

I listened to the silence of the sun as it crept up the backside of the earth and peeked over the hills.

You hear your own inner voice as you read this story.

I tried. I really tried. I wanted you to know how magnificent the sunrise was this morning. But as I read back over my words, I am convinced that sunrises aren't for telling. They're for experiencing. The way red mixes with orange and pink can never be adequately described. It has to be seen. It has to be experienced. I can write about the sunrise — describe it in minute detail — and you will still miss the impact of this morning. It has to be experienced to be truly understood.

God is like that too. He who is greater than any sun or its risings invites humanity into His royal presence to taste, to touch, and to know that *He is,* and that He rewards those who seek Him. Morning after morning this town Crier calls: "Hey! Turn around, and look behind you. You're so busy driving west, toward work and money and bosses, that you're missing it. You're missing Me. You're missing the only Lord the world will ever know."

Words about the sunrise can be inspiring, beautiful and lyrical expressions. But they will never take the place of *seeing* a sunrise, experiencing its majesty and magnificence. Nouns and verbs cannot be tasted or touched or seen. They can only be read. They are merely words.

And it is not enough to read about the Lord of Heaven and know that He exists. God desires people who will devote themselves to pausing daily and noticing that each moment of life with Him is filled with rich, wonderful color and sound and His presence. Hear His voice. Listen as He issues a sensory summons that rings and sings and brings with it an invitation to the most intimate relationship—a personal, vital, firsthand experience with the Living God.

"Taste and see that the Lord is good."

Psalm 34:8

THE TRAIN RIDE

If you talk to my son today — my oldest son, who loves his dad and at twenty-one, still kisses his mother goodnight — if you ask him about being frightened and alone and lost, he will tell you this story. And as he tells it, you will notice his eyes flash in reminiscence, and you will know he will never forget.

SAN FRANCISCO IS a beautiful city, and when my parents came to visit us from the Midwest, we wanted to show them around its lovely haunts. We drove from our home in central California to the Bay Area and parked our car in a rapid transit parking lot. We would ride BART (Bay Area Rapid Transit), a train that travels under the bay and into San Francisco.

Preparing for an all-day trip is not easy with two small children. My wife had packed extra diapers, a fold-up stroller, and blankets to protect baby Nathan from the cold winds that so often blow off the bay. She also packed snacks for Marcus, who was three-and-a-half and always hungry. She dressed him in his brown trench coat and hat that tied under his chin, and made his auburn hair shine like silk. When we got to the parking lot, all six of us got out of the car—my parents, Randee and me, baby Nathan, and Marcus.

This was our first time to ride BART. As initiates, we stood in front of the automated ticket machine and read every word of the instructions. Some of the seasoned riders behind us looked annoyed and wished we would forego our running dialogue.

Me: Let's see now. We want to go to Embarcadero Center. That's on that orange line on the map over there. So we should put in $1.85 each.

Randee: Is that one-way, or $1.85 round trip, I wonder.

Man behind us, looking at his watch: One-way, lady. It's $1.85 one way. If you want to come back, it'll cost you another $1.85 each.

It wasn't *his* comment or glare that caused us to skip the directions and start dropping money into the machine. The people standing behind him glared at us too. They all seemed to have watches, and they looked at their watches between disgusted looks at us. Sometimes, a person just knows when to hurry. That day, we knew. And we hurried.

We stuffed dollar bills and quarters and dimes and nickels into that machine until we all had tickets to enter the terminal. And then we stuffed our newly purchased tickets into an electronic turnstile that sucked those tickets into the bowel of the machine. Like magic, the turnstile opened and gave us back our ticket so we could exit the system when we got off the train. One by one, we hurried through the opening.

We rode the train all the way to San Francisco and got off in the very center of the city. The familiar bell of a cable car greeted us as we strolled down Market Street. We hopped that cable car and rode to the Wharf.

The smells of the Wharf are particularly wonderful. We watched as men dropped crabs into stainless steel pots filled with boiling water. Within moments, they began to lift those crabs out with long-handled, wooden ladles. We listened to the crunch, as they cracked the crabs and picked out the succulent meat. We sampled too — crab cocktail with red sauce and sourdough bread.

We walked the sidewalks of Chinatown. Roasted ducks (with their heads still attached) hung upside down in windows. We took turns pushing

Nathan in the stroller and carrying Marcus — up and down and up and down the streets of San Francisco.

We decided to leave the city before 3, not wanting to get involved in the evening rush hour on our return trip. Six tired bodies went through the turnstiles and down the escalator toward the train platform below the city streets. At the bottom, we all turned left and walked to the platform to await our train, which was due to arrive soon.

Randee carried the diaper bag and a few things we had purchased on our trip. I pushed sleeping Nathan in his stroller and chatted with my mom about our day. My dad stopped to notice the construction work going on inside the terminal, and Marcus was . . . Marcus? Where's Marcus?

He was not there. He was not on the train platform.

Thirty seconds. A minute. Frantic, in frenzy, I ran up the escalator looking for my son. Randee was close behind, her mother-heart racing faster than her legs. We approached the stationmaster to explain our plight. My dry tongue did not want to make words, but I forced my emotions to be still until I had delivered my plea.

"My son is lost. My son is lost. He's only three years old, and he's lost and I need your help. Please sir, can you help me find my son?"

He needed a description: age, height, weight, color of hair, clothing.

"He's three. And he's about that tall, and I don't know how much he weighs. But he has on a brown trench coat, and his brown hat that ties under his chin, and he has auburn hair. Hurry. Please hurry. He's only three."

Before I could finished my decription, the station agent was talking on his radio to other agents all along the BART line. As I gave him the description, he gave it to all the other agents.

I tried to say more, but my mouth would not. It could not. For to talk, you have to think. And I could not think of anything but Marcus . . . and Jesus. Randee stood next to me, and I turned to her. I took her hands in mine, and I bowed my head. I made my tongue loosen its grip on the roof of my mouth, and I prayed.

I prayed aloud. I prayed in earnest. Not like my prayer before I eat oatmeal in the morning. Not like my prayer before I go to sleep at night. He was *lost*. My child was lost, and urgency stepped to the front of my prayer life.

"Jesus, please help Marcus. We don't know how or where to find him, but You do. He must feel terribly alone and afraid. Help him, Jesus. Find him and bring him back. Please."

It seemed like hours, but it was only a moment.

Literally within a few seconds of concluding my prayer with my wife, a big, booming voice came over the BART public address system. It was the station agent at the next stop down the line.

"Mrs. Jones. Mrs. Randee Jones. Your son is at the Powell Street Station. You may pick him up there!"

There was no foul play, only a comedy of errors. Marcus took the escalator down below the street level with us. But instead of turning left, he turned right. A train sat waiting on the other side of the platform. Marcus assumed *that* was our train. Without noticing that we were not with him, our three-year-old child walked inside the train, the doors quickly closed behind him, and he was off — alone, except for Jesus and a train filled with strangers — toward the Powell Street station.

I ran. Randee ran. We needed very little help from the escalator going back down, as we raced toward the train platform below the city streets. We hopped the first train that came by and rode to the Powell Street station. Waiting in the arms of the security officer was Marcus. Tan trench coat. Brown hat that tied under his chin. Auburn hair shining like silk. His face was red and wet — swollen from crying. He reached out for us and with a shaking, frightened voicc said, "You guys got on the wrong train!"

There were hugs and kisses and reunion all the way back across the bay that day on the train. Marcus sat on my lap, with one arm wrapped around my neck. He didn't say much. Quiet. But after many moments of deep, "glad-to-be-sitting-on-your-lap-Dad" breathing, he spoke.

"Dad. What would you do if you didn't find me today? What would you do if I stayed lost?"

Marcus' memory of being *lost* needed a response. Feelings of separation and desperation were close to the surface and my three-year-old was listening for some assurance. I thought for only a second, and then I hugged him even more tightly as I whispered in his ear. "Marcus, if I hadn't found you, two things would have happened today. First, I would never stop crying—never. And second, I would never stop looking—never."

He turned and looked up at me, as he put both arms around my neck. "That's what I thought," he said.

There are only two kinds of people in the world—those who are lost, and those who used to be lost.

If you're lost, then this story is for you.

There is a pain in the pit of your soul that is paralyzing. It's because you're lost. Somehow you got on the wrong train, on the wrong track, going the wrong way. Fear of failure and fear of people and fear of life surround you every moment. There is a hollowness in your heart, a desperation that resonates throughout your being. Day after day, you weary from the sorrow and sadness and pain. You are lost.

Don't you know? Your Father will never stop looking, and He will never stop crying. Stop. Get off that train of futility and wait. He's as close as your next breath. Ask Him. You'll see.

If you used to be lost, but you're not anymore, then this story is for you.

Don't forget to pray today for the *lost.* Pray specifically; pray earnestly. Pray as if you had lost a son on a train, and you had no idea which way to look. Feel the isolation and despair that overwhelm them every day . . . and pray . . . as if you would never stop looking and never stop crying. They're lost . . . *lost* . . . *lost.*

APPLES

A FRIEND CALLED one afternoon to tell us that fruit trees were on sale at a local store. Randee and I had been in the market for bare-root fruit trees because we wanted to plant an orchard on some property we own in northern California. With great eagerness, we searched out the bargain-priced trees. They were outside, in the back. One look told us why they were on sale.

They looked more like sticks than trees. Two signs marked the sale. An old sign, weathered with the ink running down the side. It read,

"Bare-root trees, ready for planting."

The other sign, obviously more recent, had been crookedly stapled over the older sign. It read,

"End-of-the-season bare-root trees—
Last chance to plant!"

Most of those little trees had limbs only a mother tree could love. Some branches were broken off—others looked like they needed to be. They were all dwarf trees—"fast-growers," the tag said. Virtually all of them were leafless, lifeless examples of what not to buy and plant if you really want to grow fruit.

Sixteen. That's how many I put into our cart. I was smart. I played the percentages. I figured we wanted to plant a dozen trees, and if we bought sixteen, four could succumb, and we'd still have twelve, live, producing trees.

I watched people's eyes as we strolled to the checkout stand with our trees. I'm not sure if the pity I saw was for us or the trees. But I know pity when I see it, and I saw it that day.

It occurred to me on the way home that I had never planted an orchard before. If there were any tricks to it, I wanted to know what they were. I called my dad. He plants lots of things—he'd know the procedure.

"Not much to it," he said. "The only thing you need to remember is don't plant a $10 tree in a $2 hole."

My trees didn't cost ten bucks, I thought to myself. *But they deserve every bit as good a treatment as $10 trees.* So I hired a man with a backhoe to dig $10 holes. I told him how to get to our property, and that I had already installed an irrigation system and driven stakes in the ground where he needed to dig. He wanted more specifics.

"How big do you want the holes?" he asked.

A good question. A reasonable question.

I said, "Oh, I don't know. How does three feet sound?"

"You got it," he replied. (He didn't know much about trees, but he knew a lot about holes. Big holes. Wide holes.)

He dug them. Twelve big, wide, deep $10 holes.

On planting day, Randee and I gathered our tools, our specially formulated plant food, and our trees, and drove to our property. On arrival, we set out across our ten-acre field with great anticipation. We saw twelve mounds of dirt each about half the size of a car. The closer we got, the taller they seemed. If trees need significant holes to do well, then these trees would do very well indeed. Randee mixed up several buckets of plant food, and with motherly tenderness poured it gently around the roots of those baby trees.

It takes a long time to cover up the roots of a tree planted in a hole three feet by three feet. Shovel after shovel. Tree after tree. We planted and laughed and guessed how long it would be before we got to eat any of the apples in our orchard. We planted the twelve healthiest trees and stuck the other four in old buckets out by the barn.

That night, our tired muscles ached with an honorable pain. All we had to show for a hard day of work was a dozen scraggly trees looking very lonely and isolated in the middle of a ten-acre field — twelve trees, and a dream that someday there'd be fruit.

That was a year and a half ago. For eighteen months now, Randee and I have checked on our little trees. We've cultivated and weeded them and checked the automatic irrigation system to make sure they're getting enough water. Faithful. That's what we've been. Faithful to the orchard we planted.

Last week, we drove up to check on the trees. I walked across the field and couldn't believe my eyes. Stupid grasshoppers. They ate every leaf off of every tree. Trees can't produce fruit without leaves. Not one apple. Not one single apple on any of those trees.

True, they weren't $10 trees, but they were good trees. We took the time to dig big, wide holes so they could get a good start. We poured special nutrients into those holes before we planted the trees. We were faithful to continue caring for them as they grew. They were loved and nurtured and cultivated. So why didn't they get a chance?

Why did those stupid grasshoppers eat my trees?

I walked back across the field, kicking rocks as I went. Star Thistle stuck to my pant legs and poked my skin as I walked. *Stupid grasshoppers. Ate my trees.* I mulled and moped and marched my disgusted self across ten, bug-infested acres.

Disgusting. That's what it was. Aggravating and demoralizing and disgusting. *Stupid grasshoppers. Ate my trees,* I murmured. I walked across the barn lot and around the back side of the barn. That's when I saw it. It caught my eye. It was standing straight as a mop handle and leaning up against the barn. An afterthought of hurried husbandry. A forgotten twig stuck into a bucket of dirt. A stick with roots that did more than survive. It produced!

Round and firm and nearly perfect they were. Two of them, hanging like isolated ornaments on a Christmas tree. They were small and green — green as Granny Smith. But they were ripe.

I walked over to the little tree slowly. I stood quietly for a moment before I reached out and picked one of those small, beautiful, unexpected apples. I polished it on my shirt as I walked toward the shade of a nearby tree. I sat down on an old combine, and I ate me an apple. Not a big apple. Not a store-bought apple. But it was one of the best apples I ever ate. And I pondered about how things grow.

How about you? Have you spent a lot of time planting something and then watching the stupid grasshoppers of life eat it before it ever had a chance? Did you do all you could to make it grow? Did you measure it and stake it and dig $10 holes? Did you irrigate and cultivate and even ask God for a little miracle?

Well, as you come walking back across the field of your unmet expectations, take a glance at a guy sitting on an old combine eating an apple. Sometimes, finding fruit is a matter of looking in the right place. The best fruit can be seemingly insignificant, growing in obscure, impossible ways. But it's there. In His time, in His way, in His power, the fruit that God grows in your life will continue, season after season. It may not happen the way you thought or where you expect, but it will happen. It *is* happening. Working in the Owner's vineyard guarantees a crop. His wisdom and strength *will produce* succulent fruit for His glory. It's just that sometimes the fruit is being produced in a place you never expected.

"So neither he who plants nor he who waters
is anything, but only God, who makes things grow."

1 Corinthians 3:7

112

ROY

I FIRST MET ROY when I was twenty-five. He was the founding pastor and senior minister at a church in Modesto, California. I was a young pastor looking for a place to serve. One sunny April afternoon, he extended an invitation to me to serve on the staff of Neighborhood Church. He has been my mentor ever since. No book on God in the neighborhood of my life could be complete without a story about Roy.

I knew he was a rare bird almost from the beginning of our working relationship. He demonstrated a humility and servanthood and wisdom I struggled to understand. I followed him around — listening and watching — and I learned.

The Oakland A's were in the World Series, playing the Cincinnati Reds. Northern California exploded with excitement at having a team in the series, and tickets were hard to come by. Roy walked into my office one afternoon and sat down.

In his hand was a ticket to the World Series.

"Jones, do you like baseball?" he said.

"Pastor, I love baseball. I'm a St. Louis Cardinal fan."

"Well," he said, "I do too. Someone gave me this ticket to the game tomorrow night. I'd like you to have it. I'll stay here and do the Wednesday night Bible study and excuse you from your regular duties so you can go."

After he walked out of my office that day, I sat there for thirty minutes thinking about what he had done. Someone had given him a ticket to the World Series. He could have easily accepted it and assigned me the duty of Wednesday night prayer meeting. He was the senior pastor. He should be the one to go. Instead, he put me first.

During my first few years at Neighborhood Church, there was much construction going on. The church needed a new facility, but finances made conventional methods of building impossible. For that reason, the new 750-seat sanctuary was built entirely with volunteer and pastoral labor. Roy led the congregation in giving all he had to the construction. Day after day, night after night he would work. He would come to the building site dressed in grubby clothes, ready for hard carpenter work. And I would try to keep up with him, work alongside him. He never complained or seemed to mind doing the work. I, on the other hand, hated it.

On one particular afternoon, we were tying steel reinforcing rods with wire, preparing to pour concrete for a wall. The wire was sharp, and the steel we handled was cold in the winter fog of California's Great Central Valley. My mind was not on servanthood or ministry as I tied the steel. I was much too busy being a victim.

Why do I have to stand on this wall tying steel twenty feet off the ground? I thought to myself. Roy worked tirelessly next to me, saying nothing. *Why do I have to do this kind of work, while the ministry inside of my office is piling up?* My conversation with myself continued. Roy, of course, couldn't hear my thinking to myself and didn't look up.

My cold hands could not hold onto the pliers I needed to tie the wire, and I accidently dropped them twenty feet to the ground. Now, I would have to climb down, pick them up, and climb all the way back up to my spot on the wall. I was disgusted.

"I'd just like to know why God is so interested in teaching us patience," I said, aloud this time as I walked to the end of the scaffolding to begin my descent down. Roy didn't look up. He said nothing. He continued to work.

I climbed down, picked up those stupid pliers

115

and dragged my weary body back up the ladder. When I reached Roy's side, neither of us spoke for probably five minutes. As Roy finished his row and started to climb off the scaffold, he turned to me and quietly answered my earlier question. "Jones, I think He's interested in teaching us patience because that's the way *He* is, and He wants us to be like Him."

I thought about what he said the rest of the afternoon. *He's interested in teaching us patience because that's the way He is, and He wants us to be like Him.*

Month after month I watched his life. Year after year I listened to his wisdom, and I loved and admired him. We got together as a staff for breakfast once a week just to talk about how things were going. On one particular morning, my mouth was moving faster than my brain. I was in rare form. My young pastor-mind theologized about growing in the Christian walk, and how I believed it was possible, if Christians *really* applied themselves, to learn certain lessons about God without His having to take us through deep waters. "Why," I said, "couldn't we just learn to trust without being exposed to all those difficult things? If we *truly* trusted God, He wouldn't have to subject us to trials."

Roy had just finished his eggs and bacon. He

pushed his plate away, put his old, green hat on his gray, wrinkled head and looked at me for a moment before he stood to leave the restaurant. Then he spoke, and I listened.

"Jones, you'll never amount to anything for God until you've been broken in a thousand different pieces . . . a thousand different times." With that pearl, he dropped a tip near his plate and slowly walked out the door.

I sat in the booth of that restaurant thinking about what he had said until the waitress finally ran me out, nearly an hour later. The musicality of his wisdom, and the lyric of truth in what he said kept running through my mind like a song you can't get out of your head: *Broken in a thousand different pieces . . . a thousand different times.*

I did not ask his permission to include a story about him in this book. Had I asked, his humble spirit would have chided me for mentioning him. But I have taken literary privilege because of what I have seen in his life. Or perhaps I should say, *Whom* I have seen in his life.

God has always enjoyed watching men walk together, the young learning from the old. He let Joshua traipse up the mountain after Moses. He let Elisha tag along with Elijah. He let Barnabas and Timothy follow Paul around. There must have been days when they sat and scratched their heads after listening to the old apostle preach and teach.

If you're a young man or woman, look around the neighborhood of your life. Somewhere within earshot, there is an older, wiser one, who has been weathered by life and storm—seasoned by trials of waiting and hoping and trusting. Talk to them. Listen to them. Watch them. Emulate their faith and follow them as they follow Christ.

If you are an older believer and you've walked in the Way for many years, the repository of your faith is a gold mine to those who are just learning the *walk*. Look around for a young man or woman who's never been to the World Series in your neighborhood, and you've got just the ticket. Watch for younger ones growing impatient with the journey. Tell them of times when you were impatient and what you learned. They need the wisdom you have earned.

And if you happen upon a young, impetuous pastor-type, who makes brash statements that he hasn't thought through, be patient and kind, and by all means, feel free to pass along the pearl that my mentor and pastor and friend dropped in my lap one day: *You'll never amount to anything for God until you've been broken in a thousand different pieces . . . a thousand different times.*

I love you, Roy.

THE SIGN

YESTERDAY, I TOOK a drive. It wasn't a long drive. In fact, I drove only about twenty minutes from my home. I turned off the freeway just after I went through the Caldecot Tunnel going west toward the Oakland hills. The area looked like a war zone. Just a few weeks ago, a firestorm consumed thousands of acres and thousands of homes in the East Bay hills of Oakland.

I drove through what used to be beautiful neighborhoods with lovely trees and impeccably kept yards. Street after street. Block after block. All that was left of those beautiful homes was piles of rusty metal on empty lots and concrete drives that led to nothing.

I read the signs as I drove along — many signs, homemade and hand-printed — about lost pets in the fire storm. There were pictures of beautiful animals on the signs; cats and dogs that had once been members of families, faithful pets now missing and being sought. Rewards offered. Laments expressed on paper—blue flyers nailed to power poles about "General," a Black Lab who hadn't been seen since that awful Sunday it all began.

Another sign was carefully lettered in bright red paint and wired around a beautiful, old, oak tree sitting at the entrance to an empty lot: *This tree is being saved. Do not harm.*

The most interesting signs I saw on my drive yesterday, however, were obviously professionally printed and mass-produced for homeowners in the area. They were white signs, about two-feet by three-feet, with bright blue lettering. There were hundreds of them throughout the devastated neighborhoods. They were nailed to posts and fences and trees. They were stapled to anything left standing, anything permanent: *"This property is* **not** *abandoned. It is* **under the control of the owner."**

I understood, of course, the meaning of the sign and why it was necessary. Some people in our society feel that when tragedy strikes, they have the right to pick up the pieces and call those pieces their own. The authorities call that looting, and it is illegal.

But I could not help being intrigued by the wording of the sign. Not the first part. Not the part that said, *This property is not abandoned.* People just don't walk off and leave a place they call *home* just because a fire storm incinerated everything in its path for five miles. People are resilient and defiant. Even though it had only been a few weeks since the disaster, I could see some of them already starting to doggedly rebuild their homes. I understood perfectly the first part of the sign.

The part of the sign that intrigued me was the second part—the part that said, *It is under the control of the owner.* I felt an eerie sense of sorrow as I read that statement.

Their property was not under their control. It had never been under their control. Eight weeks earlier, a fire storm had swept through this neighborhood. Residents grabbed the few belongings they could (if there was time) and frantically fled through the winding canyon roads. Some of them lost their pets. Most of them lost their homes and valuables, and some of them even lost their lives. They were frightened and disoriented and absolutely out of control.

Within days after this terrible happening, they returned. They regrouped and resolutely set about beginning again. And one of the first things they did was post signs—to indicate they were in control of their lives and their property and their future.

Signs have always been important to us. That must be why God peppered the neighborhood with them. After one particularly devastating rain,

He placed a rainbow—a sign and a promise that the water would never get that deep again.

Later on, He drew a sign for the shepherds. "Here's a sign for you," He said. "You'll find the Babe wrapped in swaddling clothes and lying in a manger." Such an obvious sign, easy to read with bold lettering. Control was being reestablished. It was time to announce the construction of a house not built with human hands.

A little more than thirty years later, construction was almost done, another sign was made. Crude and vile was the sign nailed over the Carpenter's head. It was not ambiguous. It was simple and plain and easy to understand: "This is Jesus, King of the Jews."

Priceless crown of thorns for the Prince of heaven; bleeding, dying Pauper of peace who never owned a home, putting the final touches on a new way to live. . Suffering Servant with a sign over His head, proclaiming to the world once and for all that the devastation had been overcome and permanent residence for all who believe had been established. The Owner had wrapped His love-message around an old cross, sturdy as an oak:

This Property Is **Not** Abandoned;
It Is **Under the Control of the Owner.**

MRS. PACK

TUCKED IN THE "remember box" of my wife's cedar chest is a picture of Simeon, standing in front of our house wearing a brand new backpack. He was five years old when the picture was taken. He wore a new yellow shirt and new jeans and tennis shoes. In fact, I think every article of clothing he wore that day was fresh from the store and barely had the tags taken off. The picture of Simeon was taken on the first day of school — the *very* first day of school for our youngest son.

I had almost forgotten, but along with the picture of Simeon, tucked away in the "remember box" was a letter I wrote to his kindergarten teacher. I pinned the note to Simeon's shirt as he walked out the door on that momentous morning. I had almost forgotten that event, but seeing the picture and reading the letter caused me to appreciate the reason my wife keeps a box of rememberings.

Simeon's kindergarten teacher was Mrs. Pack. She loved children. I think every kindergarten teacher I ever met loved children. But when I say Mrs. Pack loved children, I mean she *loved* children in an extraordinary way. She had a unique way of making three-foot-tall people feel like they were whole and important and able to do incredible things because Jesus had created greatness in them.

Jesus was the very center of all she taught. He came to class with her every day. Because she taught in a Christian school, He was the theme of her bulletin boards. He was the One who made the fall leaves change color. He was the One who turned winter into spring. When the Thanksgiving feast was held in her class, and half of the kids were Indians and the other half were Pilgrims, Mrs. Pack was quick to point out that God was the reason for Thanksgiving, and that He was the One who created both the Pilgrims and the Indians.

There were lots of opportunities to visit Mrs. Pack's kindergarten class the year Simeon was attending. She would invite parents to join the class for lunch occasionally, and when our turn came to visit the class, Randee and I enjoyed watching a master teacher as she led the parade of five- and six-year-olds around the room. The children set the table for lunch, and when it was time to pray, Mrs. Pack led the group in a song and prayer that convinced me she wanted more than the food to be blessed. She really wanted the children to be blessed too.

During our stay in the classroom that afternoon, an ambulance happened to pass the school, its red light flashing, its siren blaring. Mrs. Pack stopped her lesson about the difference between *p* and *b* at the chalkboard, folded her hands, bowed her head, and led the class in prayer: "Jesus, it sounds like someone is in trouble. We don't know who they are, but You do. Please help whoever that is. If they are hurt, take care of them. If they are sick, heal them. If they are afraid, help them know You are there with them. Amen." Then she turned immediately back to the board and her lesson about the difference between *p* and *b*. Letters and sounds and words were important to Mrs. Pack, and she said they were important to Jesus too. But not as important as people.

On the last day of school, Mrs. Pack scheduled a picnic for all of the children in her class and their families. It was an elaborate affair, held out in the country at the home of one of the children. I had heard from other parents that this was an event not to be missed, and our entire family went. We ate barbequed hot dogs, potato salad, and drank red sickeningly sweet punch that gave all the kid red mustaches. We had chocolate cupcakes with white icing that the kindergartners had decorated themselves. But the food wasn't the reason we came. We came to celebrate the end of a great year—the first year of school for our children.

After we ate, there was an awards ceremony. Mrs. Pack gave awards for everything—lots and lots of awards. Every child in the class came away from that ceremony with a fistful of awards and certificates for being "the best paper picker-upper in the class," or "the person who nearly always sits with their hands folded and their desk cleared off *before* the final bell rings." There were no losers. There was much clapping and smiling and congratulating as the afternoon wore on. Parents were obviously proud of their kids, who had grown more inside than out in nine, short months.

After the awards ceremony, Mrs. Pack brought out the rope. It wasn't a clothesline rope. It was one of those ropes elephants pull to put up the tent in the circus. It was two inches thick, strong, and long, and *perfect* for a tug-of-war.

"It's time for our annual tug-of-war," she said. I supposed she would pit the boys against the girls or the Red reading group against the Blue reading group. Not Mrs. Pack. She had a much better idea.

"I want all the dads to line up on this side," she said, as she pointed to the left side of the lawn. "And I want all my big kindergartners who will be going into the first grade next year to line up on the right side of the lawn." One of the things that I had learned in being around Mrs. Pack was that when a direction was given, there were no questions asked. Obedience was expected; obedience was given. The group of dads lined up on the left side of the lawn, looking like men lined up to punch a time clock for work, as Mrs. Pack pulled the thick rope across the grass.

"If there are any other boys and girls who would like to join the kindergartners, you may do so," she said. Now, another fifteen or so children joined the kindergarten team.

"Dads, this will be a demonstration to show how strong your children are. Please take hold of the rope, and when I give the signal, try to pull the children across the lawn. Do your best. Don't hold back. Try to pull them across the lawn."

Our side — the dad side — had about eight or nine men. We took the rope in our hands, while Mrs. Pack walked to the other side — the kindergarten, kiddy side. She said something to them, but I couldn't hear what it was. She was smiling. She was coaching. She excited the children with what she said, and they grabbed the rope like they were stevedores about to move the Queen Mary into its birth.

"When I count three," Mrs. Pack said, "When I

count three, I want both sides to pull with all your might. Ready? One ..."

I could see in the faces of some of the dads that they though this was going to be easy.

"Two ..."

I looked across at the kiddy team, and I saw a determined Simeon — my Simeon — holding the two-inch rope in his small hands. Simeon did not look big enough to hold such a large rope.

"Three!"

The contest had begun. The rope pulled taut, like a giant bowstring. The knuckles on the hands of this dad turned white and tight. Feet dug into the lawn on both sides of the rope, and the contestants leaned back, leveraging their weight, tugging and pulling.

A line of grown men moved. It moved from left to right. The dads were being pulled across the lawn. Like pistons, the tiny legs and feet on the other end of the rope dug into the lawn, getting traction and footing, and they walked backward across the lawn.

There was a genuine attempt on the part of the dads — this dad — to stop the movement, but it was futile. Mrs. Pack's pack of kindergartners had pulled us across the lawn, with very little effort.

I wouldn't have believed it. If I hadn't been there, I wouldn't have believed that those twenty-five-or-so children could outpull eight or nine grown men. But they did. I would never have thought that one little lady could excite a group of children so much that they believed they could move the world—but she did.

I don't know what Mrs. Pack said to those kids on the other side of the rope that day at the annual end-of-the-year picnic. She may have reminded them of the story of David and Goliath. She might have reminded them that Jesus multiplies things like loaves and fishes, when children are willing to give all they have.

I don't know what she said to those children on the last day of school. But I know what I said to Mrs. Pack on the first day day of school, as Simeon walked out the door in his new yellow shirt and brand new backpack. I know what I said because I wrote it down and my wife was wise enough to put it in her box of rememberings.

Dear Mrs. Pack,

Well, it's finally happened. Our third little boy walked bravely out the door this morning—out of the safety and security of our constant protection—into a new world filled with fears, tears, laughs, and perhaps most of all, a world of tremendous challenges.

This morning, what is "old hat" to a veteran like you will be the experience of a lifetime for us. Randee and I are sending you our little boy, our only *youngest* son. At the end of this day, the boy who returns will not be that same little boy, but instead, the beginnings of a young man.

As parents, we look forward to participating with you in the education of Simeon this year, as he discovers new and exciting things. But we have already prepared ourselves for the fact that a new room has been opened in Simeon's heart that can only be occupied by "Teacher," that strange mixture of tenderness, love, discipline, and knowledge that causes a child to learn and grow.

Thank God you are there, and that you know in a personal way the risen Christ. What would we do if we were sending our Simeon across that threshold this morning to a stranger who didn't look to the wonderful Counselor for guidance?

Have a fabulous year!

Ken Jones
Simeon's Dad

THE UNINVITED GUEST

I'VE ALWAYS loved company. I grew up in a home where the front door was seldom locked, and a constant stream of friends and relatives enriched our lives with their warmth and conversation. I learned the art of hospitality by watching my parents welcome guests into our home — guests who had come with no other motive or agenda in mind but to see us and talk.

When it was time to go home, the company always seemed to know it. As the conversations died down, one of the guests would say, "Well, it's time to go. We don't want to wear out our welcome." My parents would respond to such statements with a predictable, "Don't rush off," or, "What's your hurry," but everyone seemed to know the rules for a visit: Before it becomes awkward, thank your hosts for their hospitality and then leave.

When my wife and I were first married, we continued the practice of opening our home to family and friends. Friendships, cultivated in the setting of our living room have enriched our lives, our family, and our ministry.

In the summer of 1983, however, an uninvited guest came to our door. He did not knock. He swaggered into our home unannounced and has been taking advantage of our hospitality ever since. He dominates many of our conversations. He chooses his own seat at our dining table. He has his hand in virtually every aspect of our lives and insists that we plan our everyday routines and even our vacations around him. Frequently, when I embrace my wife, or even look into her beautiful green eyes, he is there. Even our marriage bed is not a stranger to him, and he seems to take particular delight in spoiling our attempts at intimacy. He sits with us in church. He goes with us on long walks. He was not invited. He was not expected. His name is Pain. He has become an uninvited guest at our house. And he doesn't know when it's time to leave.

For most people, pain is a relative word. When a headache interrupts our usually painless life, most of us hurry to the medicine cabinet and grab a couple of aspirins. Within minutes, our acute pain has subsided, we feel better, and life goes on. However, for millions of others, chronic pain is truly a *relative* word, like a long lost cousin who drops in uninvited and unwelcome and doesn't know when to leave. That's the way it is our house.

I first noticed him when he would drop by for a casual visit, affecting and infecting my wife with his own brand of domination. She would slow down and wait for him to leave before she could resume her household chores and other wifely, motherly, teacherly duties. She usually announced his presence with variations on a theme: "My legs are really hurting me today."

But in the early days it was rare for us to postpone any of our activities because Pain had dropped by for a visit. In fact, I rarely paid any attention to whether he was visiting or not. He didn't talk to me. Only to my wife.

It became increasingly apparent, however, that he was taking advantage of our hospitality. This uninvited guest frequented our home more and more often, and we decided to seek professional help to evict this pest. After nearly two years of increasing discomfort and various treatments, doctors recommended that Randee undergo fusion surgery for the herniated disc in her lower back. We hoped the operation would bring relief from her pain and let her return to a normal life. Neurosurgeons performed the delicate surgery.

For days afterward, I sat in that hospital room and held her hand. I stroked her face and told her

I loved her. But she couldn't hear me—Pain was talking to her. The corridor lights flashed at 9:00 P.M. signalling the end of visiting hours. Nurses would come and tell me—the husband—I had to leave. But Pain stayed with Randee all night.

Ten days after her surgery, we heard the good news from the doctor, "You can go home today." I packed her things, the nurse wheeled her down the hall, and the four of us got on the elevator— Randee and me, the nurse . . . and Pain. I brought the car to the front door of the hospital. Three of us got in and rode off together. The nurse stayed at the hospital.

And so it was that Pain came to take up permanent residency in our house. It may be that he lives at your house too.

I don't know what you think about him, that robber, that intruder, that violator who has come through your door and won't let you rest. The cause of his visit may be a herniated disk or a birth defect. It may be a car accident or an emotional breakdown. It may be alcohol or drug induced pain. But it is pain.

I don't know how you *feel* about your particular, personal pain. But I am confident that when chronic pain comes to call, he brings baggage— feelings of isolation, fear, and doubt.

I don't know what you think of Him, the Carpenter, the Storyteller, the Teacher—who spits on the ground and makes mud, then smears it on darkened eyes and they see.

I don't know how you feel about the Doctor, the Physician, heaven's Healer who shouts into deaf ears, "Be opened!' and they are.

But I will tell you how this husband and pastor feels—what I've learned about pain:

1. Pain came into my life because God opened the door. God didn't cause the pain, but I am convinced He allowed it. Why? I have no idea.

2. Life and Pain are not the same. Both are difficult, but they are not the same.

3. By seeing Pain as a person, I distinguish the one I love from the one I hate. My wife and Pain are not the same. The mother of my three sons and Pain are not the same. One is the joy of my life—the other wants to rob me of joy.

4. Some days are better than others.

5. Some days are worse than others.

6. Every day is unlike any other, and I can choose to be victim or victor—bitter or better.

7. It helps when I pray for my wife.

8. It helps when she prays for me.

9. We are learning together about not dwelling on him; he pummels the flesh, but we choose to affirm the spirit and the worth of each other.

10. Pain will not stay forever. He will be evicted one day by the Guest of honor who sits at the head of our table and our lives. He who does all things well will perform it. It may not be today . . . but someday.

"Now the dwelling of God is with men,
and He will live with them.
They will be His people,
and God Himself will be with them and be their God.
He will wipe every tear from their eyes.
There will be no more death or mourning
or crying . . .
. . . or pain."

Revelation 21:3-4

AL AKIMOFF

THE BEAUTY OF HOLLAND raced by the window of the train as I prayed silently for God's help. I was in a strange land, speaking only English, on the way to Amsterdam to make contact with Al Akimoff. Al, a friend from Bible college days, was serving as a missionary in Europe. When I called him from the States a few months earlier, he sounded excited to be able to loan us a van for the seven-week concert tour I was leading to U.S. military installations. He had given me three phone numbers in Amsterdam. I was to call when I landed with the team in Brussels.

I had spent nearly a week in Brussels trying to reach Al by telephone, but no one ever answered. If I could not contact him soon, our entire itinerary would be in jeopardy. I decided to make the trip from Brussels to Amsterdam and somehow try to find my friend. Now, I sat on a train, admiring the lovely countryside of Holland and praying that

God would help me.

The train seemed to stop at every little hamlet along the way to Amsterdam, picking up various travelers who spoke to each other in Dutch or German. At one stop about thirty minutes outside of Amsterdam, a young man boarded the train and sat down next to me. He had a pleasant expression on his face as he looked my way and began speaking in Dutch. I smiled and shook my head, trying to let him know I didn't understand a word he was saying.

"Oh, you speak English?" he said. "Then I'll just speak English too."

It was obvious this jolly young man of twenty-five or so wanted to talk, and he quickly engaged me in a discussion about what I was doing on a train headed for Amsterdam. I told him I was on a musical trip, leading a group of singers who were waiting for me back in Brussels.

I said, "We sing Gospel music, and we have concerts scheduled on military bases throughout Europe."

"Then you must be a Christian," he said, sitting up and turning more toward me. He extended his hand to me and said, "I'm very pleased to meet you, Brother."

For the next several minutes, we each shared our stories—first his and then mine. He was traveling throughout Europe for the summer, wanting to see some of the world. His home was in Canada, and he said he met Christ in a Christian & Missionary Alliance church. I briefly told him the rest of my story—that I was going to Amsterdam to find my friend who was to help us with a van, that I had been unable to reach him by phone and had no idea where he was.

My new friend asked how he could help.

"Do you know how to use these phones?" I asked. He assured me that he did, and as the train rolled up to the Amsterdam station, I breathed a sigh of relief, thanking the Lord for sending someone to help me in my dilemma. We walked outside the train station to some pay telephones. He dialed the number, while I prayed silently.

The first number—no answer. We let it ring twenty times. With each ring, my heart sank deeper. I decided to try the second number.

On the second ring, a voice on the other end said, "Hello," in very broken English.

"Yes, my name is Ken Jones. I'd like to speak to Al Akimoff."

"Al is not here. He has not been here in weeks. I have no idea where he is."

I thanked the gentleman and then turned to my newfound brother in Christ, who was still standing next to the phone booth. We had one more number to try.

"Would you mind if we pray before we try this last call?" I said. "If I don't reach Al Akimoff today, I'm afraid I don't know what I'm going to do."

He agreed, and together we bowed our heads and prayed, standing next to the Amsterdam train station. It was a short prayer. It was a "God, do something quick" prayer. I felt no earth-shattering response from heaven. I sensed nothing out of the ordinary at all, in fact. I only knew I was totally dependent upon God.

When we finished our prayer, I gave my new friend the last number I had for Al Akimoff. He dialed, conversed with the operator in Dutch for a moment, and then handed me the phone, saying, "It's ringing now."

I took a deep sigh and put the phone to my ear, turning to lean on the shelf in the phone booth. I stared out the side glass of the phone booth while the phone continued to ring. That's when I noticed. That's when I lost my composure. Standing in the next phone booth to mine, holding a phone to his ear, and looking me straight in the face, was my old friend from Bible school days, Al Akimoff.

I dropped the phone in my booth, leapt out the door, and grabbed him. I lifted his small frame completely off the ground, jerking the phone he was trying to use from his hand. I hugged him and told him it was a miracle. I could hardly believe it. God had led me to the exact phone booth Al would be using at precisely the same time and day. Neither of us had any idea the other was there until that exact moment.

I introduced Al to my new friend, who stood watching, smiling, pleased to be part of something so special. After I thanked him, the young man walked into the crowded streets of Amsterdam, as Al and I continued to marvel at our miraculous experience.

I don't remember what that young man looked like, and I don't recall his name, only the fact that he helped me with the strange phones in Amsterdam, and that he prayed with me on a street corner outside of the train station that morning.

Sometimes, when I tell this story, people ask me if I think the young man was an angel. I choose not to think so. I choose to think he was a young believer who allowed himself to be used as a willing servant of God.

And I choose to believe that God has a tremendous sense of humor **and** a wonderful sense of timing. He happened to be in the neighborhood of the Amsterdam train station that day and couldn't resist the opportunity of watching two old friends renew their acquaintance over a phone.

NAMES

RETURNING TELEPHONE calls is one of my least favorite things to do, not because I don't like people, but because talking on the telephone is my *very* least favorite thing to do.

Talking on the telephone is not as bad as having to change a flat tire, I suppose; not as frustrating as going back to a gas station to see if they found my gas cap. It's not that bad . . . but almost.

A few weeks ago, I received a long-distance call. I was out of the office at the time, and the message was to call operator six. Reluctantly, I picked up the phone and dialed.

"Operator six, please" I said.

In a moment, a cordial lady came on the line, and I gave her the information on the call I was trying to return.

She said, "And your name?"

A simple question, with a simple answer.

"Jones," I said. "Ken Jones."

That's when it happened. That's when she asked me — innocent and routine and standard procedure, I suppose — a question she had already asked a zillion times that day. But this time, without pause or hesitation, she asked me a question I had never been asked in my entire life.

She said, "Could you give me the correct spelling of your last name, please?"

"Spell *my* last name?" I said. "Ma'am, I've been waitin' all my life for somebody to ask me how to spell my last name. It's J-O-N-E-S. No frills, No flash, Just plain *Jones.*"

I don't remember whose call I was returning that day. I don't even remember what it was about. But I remember that operator — operator six. She's the one who asked me about my name, and when you have a name like *Jones,* you almost never get asked about your name.

When you grow up with a name like *Jones,* and you are in the third grade, and Miss Jordan assigns seats on the first day of class, you *know* where you are going to sit for the rest of the year, before she tells you. You are going to sit somewhere in the middle.

Miss Jordan seated everyone alphabetically. That meant Ben Allen was going to be in the first seat. Miss Jordan was predictable in that sense. And she was meticulous too — especially about spelling.

"Ben, is the correct spelling of your name with one "l" or two. Ben sat down in the very front row, the very first seat, and said, "One *A* and two *l*s."

When you had a name like Jones, you never got to sit in the backseat, either, away from the glaring eyes of Miss Jordan. That seat was always for Ron Yates. For the next nine months, he got to sit back there with Janet Rhinc and pass notes and eat sunflower seeds and have fun.

Me? I was in the middle. I was in the third row and the third seat — right where Miss Jordan stood when she talked about the Pilgrims and the first Thanksgiving. My seat was the fulcrum of the class when she lectured about balance and levers during science.

My desk sat right in the middle, so when the teacher let the front of the alphabet go to the lunchroom first, I had to wait for half of the kids in class before my turn came. Sometimes, she wanted to be fair, and she started with the end of the alphabet, so Ron Yates got to go first. That lucky dog. He got the best seat in the class, and he even got to go to recess first once in a while.

But me? I was in the middle — third row, third seat. Miss Jordan never once in nine months looked at me, and said, "Kenny Jones, you've been so patient. Today we will start with the *J*s. You can go first." The reason, of course, was that I sat in the middle, and people in the middle rarely get to be first.

I do not recall any teacher ever asking me for the correct spelling of my name either. Such a common name. Such a simple, short, easy to say name. Everyone knows how to spell *that* name. Everyone knows how to spell *Jones.*

In high school, I heard teachers ask Marie Fryntzko about her Serbian name. They'd stumble over its pronunciation and say it slowly several times so they'd remember it. *Fryntzko* is hard to say.

I've heard people ask Ward Tanneberg about his name. He's my friend—one of my very best friends. And he has a Danish name. I know people ask him where his name came from, because I've heard them. I've heard them ask him to spell his name slowly and clearly, so they'd get it right. But people don't do that with *Jones.* They don't need to, because everyone knows how to spell *Jones.*

Everyone knows how to spell *God* too. Such a common name. Such a simple, short, easy-to-say name. Everyone knows how to spell *that* name.

It's such a common name that people take liberties. They attach vulgarities and obscenities to that name without a second thought. They blaspheme and blame and belittle that name.

They don't let Him sit in the very front seat of their lives. That's for the *A*s—the top priorities, the plans and ideas and dreams that don't take a back seat to anyone or anything. They're not nervy enough to send Him to the back row. They still think of Him sometimes. They still know He's there. But He's *always* there. Familiar, easy, and His name is as common as *Jones*.

And so, many people put God in the third row, third seat of their lives. The One who is *Alpha* and *Omega,* the *First* and the *Last,* the One who is from everlasting to everlasting. They send Him, like a third grade school boy, to be lost in the anonymity of the third row.

That ought not to be. He deserves better. His sacrifice deserves better. His name deserves a higher place of honor, because . . .

"Holy and awesome is His name."

Psalm 111:9

THE BACK OF
THE LINE

YESTERDAY, MY WIFE and I went on a date. We decided to see a movie, and after we were seated in the theater, I went to get some popcorn. I stood in line for almost fifteen minutes. But I did more than just stand. I listened. I faced the front of the line and listened, as behind me two ladies talked.

They talked about their children. One of them was having trouble with her teenage son. He was keeping late hours and wouldn't tell her where he was. Money was a problem, she said. Going to movies was a rare form of recreation. She mentioned her loneliness. She was glad to be with her friend and "away from things" for a while. I didn't turn around to see her face, but her voice sounded pressed, serious, and burdened.

The other woman had two children — a ten-year-old daughter and a younger son who joined them as we waited and told his mother to "hurry it up, will ya?" The woman said her daughter used to get good grades and keep her room clean. But now, all she wanted to do was listen to that awful rock music. She said her kids fight like cats and dogs. There was no mention of a husband, so I assumed she was a single mom. She didn't have enough money to make the rent payment next week. Her boss was really giving her a hard time, and if she didn't need the job so badly, she'd quit.

The women remarked several times how slowly the line was moving. "Why don't they hire some more help?" one of them said. The other responded, "Yeah. With this many people in line, they need ten people behind the counter waiting on customers. This is ridiculous!" They looked around me toward the front of the line and wished out loud that "the movie would start, so all these people would go inside and sit down. Then we'd be in the front of the line."

I felt sad for those two ladies. I could hear the weariness in their voices. *When would the hard part be over? How much longer until things smoothed out and life got easier?* The words they used to describe their lives were not exciting words. These two sad women took turns describing their colorless days— pallid, sallow lives, plain and ordinary and monotonous.

They hoped for a respite. They longed for a

shorter line. And I just stood and listened as we inched our way forward.

The desire to be in the front of the line seems to be a common theme for human beings, doesn't it? We have a natural proclivity toward forming lines, and all of us hope we get a spot close to the front. That must be why God mentioned the little guy in the back.

He couldn't see. He was short, and even on his tiptoes, he couldn't see over the heads of all those people standing in front of him. The line of people crowding in to see the Master was long and deep. Like fans watching a celebrity, hoping to get an autograph, they pushed and shoved their way to the front of the line. But life had handed him an abbreviated frame; small, short, and unable to see over the crowd.

I'll bet it was quite a sight. That tiny, grown man shinned up a sycamore tree in broad daylight. He couldn't see, and rather than miss out on the parade of the century, he climbed a tree.

We know the end of the story, of course. We know that Jesus saw Zaccheus perched in that sycamore tree. We know that the Lord invited Himself to his house for a bite to eat.

But wouldn't it have been great if someone had noticed the little guy standing in the back of the crowd—the small, seemingly unimportant person, trying desperately to catch a glimpse of God in the neighborhood? I wonder what would have happened if someone standing in the front row had said, "Here, my friend. You're having trouble seeing way back there, so I'll move over, and you can stand in front of me. I don't want you to miss seeing Jesus walk by."

I wonder what those ladies would have thought, if I had said, "Excuse me, gals, but I couldn't help overhearing your conversation. Why don't you take my spot in the line? I can wait another few minutes. It's no big deal to me, and I don't want you to miss the show because you're waiting in the back of the line. Oh, and here's my card. Give me a call next week. I'd like to give you a hand with next month's rent and try to encourage you about your kids."

It's true that God sees us wherever we are and knows exactly what we need, even when we feel like we're at the end of the line. But I can't help but think He longs for His people to notice the bedraggled ones in the back. We who are light need to penetrate the darkness and extend our hand of hope. I believe He longs and yearns for people to let the little guys stand in the front. Standing in the back of the line is more difficult for some of us than others, and sometimes the circumstances of life make it difficult to catch a glimpse of Jesus as He walks by.

ON BEING FINE

THIS WEEK I KEPT track. As I went about my normal life, I asked thirteen people how they are doing. The whole baker's dozen told me — one at a time — that they are "fine."

One of them is an alcoholic, struggling to recover from the grip of substance abuse. He looked me right in the eye, and said, "Fine," when I asked him how he is doing. But I happen to know he's not fine. He's not fine at all, because his marriage is beginning to show the signs of dysfunction. I'm really concerned for his marriage. But of course, I shouldn't be concerned, because he's fine. He told me so.

Another person I talked to this week is facing open-heart surgery next week. His flesh tone is somewhat gray-blue from a lack of proper oxygenation. But when I asked how he is doing, he said, "Fine." He can't walk from his driveway to the front of his house without stopping for a breath

. . . but he's fine.

The man I ran into at lunch yesterday buried his mom last week, and he's fine too. She had suffered a long illness that demanded much of his time. He was very close to her, and I know he'll miss her terribly. But he's fine. I know he's fine because he told me.

I understand, of course, that in our culture, when one person asks another, "How are you doing?" the question is merely an announcement of intention. "How are you, today?" is a rhetorical question for most people, used as an opening gambit to transition from "Hello," into another part of the conversation. One person asks the expected question. The other gives the required password to proceed.

It was because I was thinking about that common routine last week, that I decided to count how many people I met who said they were "fine." I asked fourteen people, and thirteen of them said they were "fine." I did find one person though, who was not fine. Actually, I didn't find her; my wife did.

I waited in the car while Randee went into the local grocery store to pick up a few things. About twenty minutes later, she came back. Apologizing for being so long in the store, she told me this story.

She said she had seen a lady she knew in the

store. Randee asked, "How are you?" The lady's response was predictable. "Fine." The lady nodded, and smiled.

Two rows down, Randee noticed her again — over by the fresh produce. When the lady saw Randee, she came over to her. "I'm not really fine," she said. "I know the Lord wants me to share this with somebody: I'm not *really* fine." In the middle of a busy market, in the midst of carrots and beets and bags of potatoes, transparency opened the door of this lady's life.

"Both of my sons are getting divorced, my teenage daughter is two months pregnant, and the doctors just discovered a suspicious mass in my colon. I am not fine. My life is very difficult right now." Randee told me she talked to the lady for several more minutes. That's why it took so long in the store. She was listening to another human "not being fine."

Fear and doubt and disappointment are not *fine*, you know. They are painful, they are awful, they may even be necessary. But they are *not* fine.

The old prophet knew that too. He sat with his servant one day in the late afternoon sun. The form that approached him on the donkey seemed to be in a hurry. He recognized her as a woman who had shown him great kindness. And he sent his servant out to see if she was fine.

"Are you all right? Is your husband all right? Is your child all right?" She answered in a most curious way, I think, for a woman whose son had died that day at noon. She said, "Everything is all right." In essence, she said, "Fine. My life is fine."

But she continued her ride toward the old prophet. She rode right up to him. She got off of that donkey. She fell at his feet, and she wept. She opened up the window of sorrow and pain and mother-love. She told the old man she was *not* fine. The old prophet did the rest.

You can read the story for yourself in 2 Kings, chapter four, if you like. If you haven't read it in a while, I won't spoil the ending by telling you what happened. But I will tell you what happened to the lady in the grocery store who talked to Randee while they stood over the carrots.

She got hugged and affirmed and encouraged. Old prophets are hard to come by these days, but salt and light are everywhere. Keep your eyes open and listen. And don't believe it for a moment. Some people who tell you they're "fine" . . . aren't.

"With this in mind, be alert
and always keep on praying
for all the saints."

Ephesians 6:18

SATISFACTION GUARANTEED

ONE OF THE THINGS I got this year for Christmas was a telephone answering machine. I never thought I'd own one because I hate leaving messages on those things. But, when I got one for Christmas, I felt obligated to hook it up and try it out. Among the packaging and other materials included with the machine was a guarantee. But it wasn't just any guarantee. It was a *Satisfaction Guaranteed* guarantee. When I read those words, it made me pause and think.

Advertisers are constantly looking for new ways to convince me that their product will meet the deepest longings of my life. Stuff. Gadgets. Tools that will make life easier and more fulfilled. Many of these wonderful products include that phrase printed on the packaging, a phrase designed to make any red-blooded American stand up and cheer: *Satisfaction Guaranteed!*

How can they say that? They don't know me

personally. They don't know my situation. And they certainly don't know what satisfies me, so how can they *guarantee* my satisfaction? Better yet, perhaps, why would they *want* to guarantee my satisfaction?

I understand the obvious answer. One of the things that keeps manufacturers of "widgets" in business is satisfied customers. If I am satisfied with their product, I'll go back and buy that same brand. If the manufacturer guarantees my satisfaction, then I can't possibly go wrong.

But they can't guarantee my satisfaction. Not *really.*

Even God doesn't give a satisfaction guarantee. He created the most beautiful place to live anyone could imagine: the Universe. He filled it with jeweled furnishings — stars and seas and mountains and deserts. He painted landscapes that any art gallery would envy. He sculpted wonderful animals and fish in beautiful colors and textures and tones. He fashioned all forms of life, from gigantic leviathans to microscopic organisms. His attention to detail was impeccable. He provided lush, sumptuous morsels — fruits and vegetables to eat. He placed two people in the center of this paradise. And the best part about it was that everything was *complimentary.* No charge.

Hard to believe, isn't it? Adam and Eve walked

in the midst of paradise. They had their run of the place. They got to name every creature. They had all the food they could ever want. They never had to fight with their neighbors. Their wardrobe was always in style. Transportation was a cinch because they weren't going anywhere.

They didn't even have to go to church because church came to them. God would walk with them and they could talk to Him face-to-face. Can you imagine?

But even with all of that, their satisfaction wasn't guaranteed. There was only one tree on earth they could not partake of. One tree! All of creation wasn't enough. Walking and talking with God wasn't enough. Living in paradise wasn't enough. They chose dissatisfaction.

I was just thinking. How am I doing at being satisfied? What satisfies me? Is it money? No, because I always think I need just a little bit more. Is it material possession? No, because as soon as I get what I think I need, I start looking for a newer, faster, better model. I know that *things* don't satisfy, but I sure spend a lot of time and money accumulating them. I've got a garage full of widgets.

No, what really satisfies me is the only thing that will satisfy any person: a vital, daily relationship with God, who fulfills my deepest longings. Nothing short of that will ever make me truly happy.

Ever wonder what God wanted to tell Adam and Eve that day He came looking for them in the Garden? They had been out shopping for something to satisfy them, and then God called. I wonder? If Adam and Eve had had an answering machine that day, would He have left a message?

"Because Your love is better than life. . . .
My soul will be satisfied as with the riches of foods;
with singing lips my mouth will praise You."

Psalm 63:3-5

THE REMODELING

A SLOW, AUTUMN rain fell as I walked the six blocks home.

I guessed that my dad might be home when I got there. Rain often played havoc with his construction job, and "too wet to work" was a common phrase in our home when I was growing up. I guessed correctly, and as I opened the front door of our house, I saw my dad, sitting on the old, gray couch in our tiny living room. He poured over a set of drawings of a house. That was a familiar scene. He was a carpenter. And I saw him look at a lot of plans and blueprints when I was growing up.

As I walked in and laid my wet language book on the coffee table, he looked up and said, "Do you recognize this place?" I walked around the table for a better view of the drawing. It was the front elevation of a house with a large picture window in the front. The house had a porch with an overhang and a flat roof. It didn't look familiar to me, and I said so.

"Whose house is it?" I asked.

"It's nobody's house yet, because it isn't built yet. But it's gonna be ours."

"Are we gonna get a new house?" I squealed.

"Not a new house. I'm going to remodel this house," he said.

"I'm going to take a power saw and cut the front wall of our house in half. Then I'm going to take those two halves and turn them both ninety degrees out toward the street. Then, I'll build a new front on our house, with a picture window, and a new door. That will make our living room a lot bigger, and I think a lot nicer. Don't you?"

"I guess so," I said.

I was a little bit troubled by the thought that cutting the house in half would make it nicer, but I had learned from experience that my dad was a great one for cutting things in half. Once, he cut my mom's new dresser in half with a saw and built her a vanity with drawers on both sides. That job was a big one; a scary thing as far as my mother was concerned, but it turned out beautifully. Now, however, dad was actually implying he wanted to remodel the house by cutting the front of it in half.

Several months later, after plans had been submitted to the city, and permits had been issued, he started. I know exactly *how* he started because I watched him. I helped him. I was there, and I remember.

He measured. He took his hundred-foot tape measure, and he handed me the end of the tape. While I held it on the end of the foundation of our house, he walked to the other side of the house and handed the tape to my mom. Mom and I stretched that tape the entire width of our house, down low, on the foundation. He walked to the very center and made a mark with a pencil.

Then he climbed upon the roof. He took a plumb line, a string with a pointed weight tied to the end, and he unwound the weight and let it swing toward the ground as he held the string against the house.

"Now, steady the string and don't let it swing," he said. "Tell me when the point of the weight is exactly on the mark I made on the foundation."

I felt very important, as I got down on my knees so I could be sure of what I saw. I closed one eye, like I was sighting a gun.

"Over some, Dad . . . over some more . . . over some more. Stop! I think that's too far. Go back the other way . . . easy . . . easy . . . There. I think that's it. It's right on the mark."

"Good," he said. And he made a mark by the

string on top of the wall, right next to the roof. He held one end of his chalk line on that mark and dropped the other end to me. When I had stretched the line taut and placed the end of it on my mark, he pulled the line away from the wall and then let it go. Snap—a bright blue line now ran down the front of our house, exactly in the center.

Some of the neighbors who had been warned that we were planning to violate the front of our house had gathered to watch. The women looked sympathetically at my mother. Their eyes said, "I'm glad he's *your* husband and not mine," but their voices said nothing.

My dad's response to such looks reminded me of what Noah must have looked like as he climbed the ladder with a bucketful of pitch. Noah's neighbors were skeptics. But he kept right on working. So did my dad.

It took five minutes, as I recall. Maybe ten. Slowly, precisely my dad cut along that blue line. He cut the front wall of our house exactly in half. Once he started, there was no turning back. You can't "un-saw" anything. When you're using a power saw, and you're running it up the front of your house, *"Oops!"* is not a word you want to hear. You've got to be sure. You've got to be exact. And you've got to be perfect.

By the end of that day, the entire front of our house was open, exposed to anyone who cared to take a look inside. By the end of the next day, the front of the house was about half enclosed, framing for the picture window, but no glass. When the sun set on the third day, a totally new front elevation had been completed. The new door was beautiful and looked like it had always been there.

I was very proud of my dad when that weekend was over. It takes nerves of steel to run a power saw up the front of your house, with the entire neighborhood standing by, shaking their heads in disbelief. He had taken an old house and turned it into a new one. The address hadn't changed. But the house was different—forever.

* * *

Once in a while, the Carpenter says, "It's time to remodel. The house is a good one but it needs enlarging. It needs to grow." From the moment He moved in, He's had the plan. Before the foundations of the world were laid in place, He understood my life. He has been measuring and planning, determined to make the house of my life— the house He calls home—more suitable for His purposes. The plumb line of heaven has marked me—a blood-red, one-of-a-kind line that stretches taut and straight from Calvary to my heart.

Tearing out walls is dirty business. Remodeling

makes a lot of noise. The violence of ripping off the old self and putting on the new is not quiet. Sometimes it wakes the whole neighborhood. Sometimes my family and friends must watch in disbelief, wondering what on earth is going on.

There are days when I'm standing exposed, like a house whose front wall has been sawed in half. I don't like standing in the draft. I don't like being open and vulnerable. It makes me feel insecure and fearful and uncertain. The cold and damp of public exposure makes my life ache, like arthritis of the soul. But the Carpenter just smiles and patiently goes about His work. House by house, block by block, the Master Carpenter walks through the neighborhoods of the kingdom measuring and planning your life and mine. Without hesitation, He exposes and changes and moves our motives and ideas and desires. Walls of pretension and facades of self-protection are cut in half and replaced by humility and honesty and conformity to the image of Christ.

Life in the kingdom is life in a construction zone. Don't be surprised if all the remodeling makes a little noise. It's the Carpenter improving the neighborhood.

LONG ARMS

A FEW WEEKS AGO, as I waited at a stop-light, a young mother walked in front of my car, holding her small child by the hand. The child looked about three or so. The mother was definitely in a hurry to cross the street; the child was *not*. The child's feet were hitting the ground about every third step as she tried to keep up with her mother's gait. I thought, *I wonder what it's like to be led by the hand, not knowing where you're going, how long it will take to get there, or why there is such a hurry?* Mother was on a mission. I don't think she was even aware she was dragging her little girl along behind her.

A few days ago, a man came into my office. I think he felt like he was being drug along too. He shared that he was tired and felt like he was on an escalator that never stopped. He said he was fragmented and lacked focus and couldn't seem to get his bearings. He used words like *race* to describe his daily routines. He talked of *schedules* and *calendars* and *free nights.*

It was apparent to me that he was holding onto things that were dragging him across the streets of his life. His feet were only landing on the ground every third or fourth day. Weary. Harried. Tired of being tired. He seemed to say that his life was out of control. He wasn't sure *what* was doing the dragging, but some *one* or some *thing* was causing a profound weariness to overtake him. He talked like a victim — like a child whose arms were weary from being dragged to the other side of the street.

A few minutes ago, during my devotional reading, I read *her* story again. She was definitely being dragged down the street. Death had already taken her husband some years before, and now this widow of Nain walked behind the body of her son — her only son — as his dead body was carried through the streets.

My guess is, she was numb. I've never lost a child to death, but I have stood with many parents who have, and virtually all of them mention the numbness that accompanies tragedy. The widow followed the coffin, sobbing, grieving the loss of her child. She had no idea what she would do now. When her husband died, she took hope in the fact that her son would be able to care for her in her old age, but now, death had taken him too. She walked behind his coffin. She followed, as death dragged her through the streets, leading a procession of grieving, sorrow-filled lives. The old woman was a victim.

But Death made a mistake. As he stood atop the coffin of the young lad while the procession made its way through the streets, Death made a wrong turn. He didn't understand. He didn't realize that God lived in that neighborhood, and that the funeral procession marched right by the window of heaven.

When Jesus saw that Death was dragging the life of a tired, old woman through the streets, He decided that enough was enough. The Bible says that His heart went out to her, and He said, "Don't cry." He stopped the parade. He touched the coffin. He spoke to a corpse, and He gave the old woman back her son.

Three people being dragged through life. One of them was a grown man, dragged down life's thoroughfares by his own lack of control and planning. One of them was an old widow, the victim of Death, until God's Son introduced Himself to her son. And one of them was a little girl, no more than three, being dragged across the street by a parent who was in such a hurry that she didn't notice that tiny shoulder was nearly out of its socket.

It's enough to make the dad in me wonder ...*Why do all my sons have such long arms?*

THE DAD WHO SHOULD HAVE ASKED, "WHY?"

YESTERDAY, AS I SAT waiting in the airport for my wife to arrive on a flight, I peeked around the edge of my newspaper and noticed a blonde little girl leading her daddy around the waiting area. She asked many questions.

"Daddy, what's that?"

"The door to the plane is too high off the ground. They need that big ramp to reach up to the door," said Daddy.

"Why is the plane so high?"

"Airplanes are very tall. The door to the plane is very high, and so they need a ramp," said Daddy.

I went back to my reading, but my ear couldn't help noticing the scene before me. The darling little girl held her daddy's hand and waited for Mama's plane, which was a few minutes late. But she wasn't patient long. Instead of holding Daddy's hand, she began to pull away. Instead of asking questions, she began to demand things.

"I want a drink! I'm thirsty," she demanded.

Daddy obediently walked to the water fountain and held the little girl up so she could get a drink.

The little girl spotted doughnuts in a nearby coffee shop. She jerked her daddy's hand like a farmer leading a prize bull into the barn.

"I want a chocolate doughnut," she demanded.

"No, Jessica. We'll eat when Mother gets off the plane."

"I want a chocolate doughnut," she demanded—now louder with a small stomp of her foot.

He continued to reason with the child, but she continued her debate. He finally bought the girl a chocolate doughnut.

I don't know if anyone has ever estimated the number of questions a child asks a parent during the first fifteen years of life, but I'd guess thousands. Thousands of "What's that?" questions—countless "Why?" questions asked by little minds that are trying to understand their world and the way it works. But asking questions is a two-way street. There are some questions that mommies and daddies need to ask their children. I'll bet the guy I read about this morning would agree.

He was a model citizen. He loved God and stood up for what was right. He demonstrated real character and courage in difficult situations. He wasn't looking for notoriety, but it seemed to follow him around; he was a real leader.

It's too bad about his kids. He did his best to give them everything they could possibly need. His kids wore the best clothes. They had the finest teachers at their elite schools. They never knew the meaning of the word *want.* He loved his children. They were the dearest thing in all the world to him.

But, in spite of all the father tried to give them, they didn't seem to appreciate him. They were totally undisciplined. They even tried to undermine his position in the community. They betrayed his trust at every turn. One of his sons raped his own sister! Another of his sons retaliated by murdering his rapist brother. The picture the Bible paints of King David's children is one of violent, rebellious, unmanageable brats!

Even though he was a man "after God's own heart," David wasn't perfect. And a strange thing is said about him in 1 Kings 1:6, after Adonijah, his son had declared himself king. It says, "His father [David] had never interfered with him by asking, 'Why do you behave as you do?' "

Seems like a logical question for a father to ask his son. But David evidently didn't want to interfere. Maybe his heart was too tender to discipline. Perhaps he left correction to others—teachers or servants. Whatever the reason, the Bible says that even though he was "old and well-advanced in years" he had never interfered with his children.

Sometimes, I like to imagine what it would be like to walk up on the front porch of a guy like David and sit and chat about his life. I have a feeling that one of the things he'd talk about would he his kids. I wonder if he ever thought about the fact that he hadn't interfered with their little lives?

I wonder what he'd say if I could ask him how he'd have done it differently? My guess is that he'd remember days when his kids were small; days when they were in the process of growing up; days when they stomped their feet and demanded their own way, like the little girl I saw yesterday in the airport. My guess is that he'd encourage parents to ask serious questions of their kids when they stomp their feet and demand their own way — questions like, "Why do you behave as you do?"

And I think he'd say, "Don't wait until they're grown before you ask them."

"The rod of correction imparts wisdom,
but a child left to itself disgraces his mother."
Proverbs 29:15

BAD FRIDAY

Saturday
6:45 A.M.

Dear God,

YESTERDAY WAS A very bad friday, and I just
wanted to say thank You.

You know, don't You, how much I always enjoy
the annual Men's Retreat here at the church? We
scheduled the golf tournament first, and I drove
the sixty-five miles over there just to play. The
front nine holes of my game were absolutely horri-
ble. I hit two shots out of bounds on the first tee —
with everyone watching. Brand new balls. I ended
up with an eleven on the first hole. From there it
was downhill, and I finished the front with a fifty-
four. Par was thirty-five, and I scored a fifty-four!
But You read my thoughts, didn't You? You saw
how determined I was to improve, how competi-

tive I was, how tenaciously I approached the tenth tee. Did You add the score for the back nine, Lord? Thirty-eight! I shot a fifty-four on the front nine, and a thirty-eight on the back. I hate to play golf like that. So inconsistent.

The drive through the mountains was beautiful on the way home. The fall colors washed over my eyes in waves of orange and yellow and red, and I thought to myself, *God did that!*

I sang to You, didn't I? What was it? O, yes, I remember now. *"To Him who sits on the throne and to the Lamb, be praise and honor and glory and power ever more. Glory, glory to the Lamb that was slain."*

The freeway wasn't as crowded as I thought it would be. It must have been because it was only 3, and rush hour hadn't started yet. But I wish I knew why those folks in front of me slammed on their brakes so unexpectedly. I saw them in plenty of time as they were sliding and skidding, the gray-white smoke from their tires screaming that something was wrong in front of them. That's why I slowed down.

I wish I knew why the man behind me was following so closely too, and why he couldn't stop before he rear ended me. Wasn't that an eerie scene, God? As I try to remember it, even though it was only yesterday afternoon, I have a difficult time picturing it in anything other than slow motion and black and white.

I wasn't hurt. Thank You, Lord, for that. The man who hit me wasn't hurt. Thank You for that too. But he was so upset. I guess it's natural for people in accidents to be shaken, but this guy was a basket case. Remember how angry he was with me? Did You hear all the names he called me, and how he got right up in my face, screaming at me? Of course You did.

I'm really not used to having someone point a finger at me, threaten me, curse at me. You must have to listen to that kind of vile language all the time, Lord, because You hear everything. But I'm a pastor. People don't usually talk like that around pastors. They don't usually direct their abuse at pastors.

Remember what he said? He was a disabled Vietnam veteran, forty-one years old, getting ready to go on vacation, and I had ruined his life. *He* hit *me* from behind on a freeway in San Jose, and *I* had ruined *his* life. He was totally out of control, emotionally unwired.

What were You thinking, Lord? Were You pleased with the way I just stood there, my hands in my pockets while hundreds of people drove by on the freeway? You knew, didn't You? You knew I was embarrassed at being ridiculed and maligned when I hadn't done anything wrong. You watched as I just looked down at the ground, steeling myself to his abuse. Twenty minutes is a long time to be reviled, but that's how long it took for the patrolman to arrive on the scene.

Did You send the patrolman? I thought You did. That's why I said, "Thanks, Lord," when he pulled up. I am still amazed that when the officer arrived, the man who hit me was polite and kind and civil. Interesting how a little authority will change a situation like that.

I know I talked to You about this on the way home, but it's the day after now. It's Saturday morning, and I have been doing some more thinking about what happened yesterday, about my bad Friday.

Remembering *my* bad Friday sparked a thought about *Your* bad Friday, and I wanted to say thank You again.

Wasn't it about daybreak? You'd already been up all night mocked and ridiculed by soldiers. It must have been terrifying. Blindfolded, beaten, maligned, and abused. What I heard yesterday was kidstuff compared to what those soldiers unleashed on You.

Have I ever told You how much I admire the way You stood there? Your manhood and strength. Your courage in the face of that abuse.

Have I ever mentioned that I think You were a very brave man when You stood there?

The "God-You"—the One who spoke light and color and stars into existence—could have raised an eyebrow and incinerated the entire galaxy. The "God-You" was not intimidated in the least by the miserable taunts and powerless accusations of mere mortals—creatures created for Your pleasure. No, I don't believe for a moment that the "God-You" had any fear or trepidation as You stood there accused that day.

But the "Man-You"—the Man of sorrows, acquainted with grief, the "Man-You" who hungered and thirsted and wept, who got angry at money changers and impatient with hypocrites—*that* You gave an incredible demonstration on that first Good Friday. You faced the worst Friday the world will ever know, frail and vulnerable and mortal. God with a jacket of flesh pulled-over omnipotence.

I've always been in awe of Your deity. But Your humanity, Your vulnerability, Your *man-ness,* represents something I cherish very much, Jesus. All it took was one Good Friday and I was convinced. All the bad Fridays I will ever face have been overcome by You. And all things—inconsequential things like frustrating rounds of golf, nerve-racking things like accidents on the freeway—all things, even bad Fridays, work together for my good. I wonder, is that why we call it "Good Friday"?

Your adoring kid,
Ken

THE LOVE NOTE

MY MIDWEST BONES were frozen on that late January day as I boarded a plane for Bethany College near Santa Cruz, California. I would be preparing for full-time ministry there. As I buckled my seatbelt, I looked forward to seeing palm trees and the ocean.

Within days of arriving on the campus I met Randee, and my interest in palm trees and the ocean diminished immediately. She was different than other girls, I thought. Quiet and shy and deep in the things of God. We went out for coffee several times, sitting and talking about our families: hers, the Smiths; and mine, the Joneses. We talked about school and friends and the future. We talked about the Lord, who was leading us both into full-time service, and I sensed such a wonderful spirit in this girl, such a warm love for God.

My feelings for her intensified. Actually, I was

in love — severely in love. Unfortunately, she was not — at least not yet. And so I plied her with candy and flowers and notes telling of my devotion to her. She smiled and nodded and thanked me. And she seemed to notice me, but very, very gradually.

One rainy morning, I worried that Randee would not have an umbrella to walk to her 7:30 class. I got dressed, grabbed my umbrella, and waited outside her dorm until she came out. We walked together under the protection of my umbrella across the campus. We walked down the hill toward the gymnasium. We talked as we walked, about the rain and wet books and our schedules. When we arrived at the door of her classroom, she handed it to me.

A card with my name on it. She said, "I saw this and thought of you." Then she turned and walked into her class.

I ran toward the campus coffee shop with my card. When I got there, my wet fingers fumbled to carefully open the envelope without damaging its precious contents.

On the front of the card, there was a cartoon of a little girl with blonde hair, her face and hands covered with chocolate. Beneath the picture, in crayon-like, crooked printing were these words: *"I like you better than chocolate-covered graham crackers."*

I stared at the damp card for a few seconds before I looked inside. There, in the same, crayon-like printing, were these words:

*"And I **really like** chocolate covered graham crackers!"*

The card was signed **"Love, Randee"**

I leaned back and looked up at the ceiling, smiling. I just sat there in the coffee shop in wet clothes, alone with a cup of cold coffee.

I enjoyed the caption: *"I like you better than chocolate-covered graham crackers . . . And I **really like** chocolate-covered graham crackers."* I thought the sentiment and idea were terrific. But the part of the card that sent me into orbit was the handwritten part; *her* handwritten part that read: *"Love, Randee."* I thought that note — the first love note I ever got from my Randee — was the most beautiful love note I had ever read. But that was before she shared the other love note with me. It was written to Another: Someone who had captured her heart before I came along. It was obvious by reading the note that she was involved in an ongoing relationship, and that her feelings for this significant Other were deeper than her feelings for me.

She had written it on the first blank page of her Bible, from her heart, in her own hand. A vow to the Bridegroom:

"I Randee, take thee Jesus, to be my beloved Savior;
To work together under God's holy ordinance.
I will love You, worship You, honor You,
forsaking all others.
But keep You only to myself, I cannot.
I will share Your love with those who need it most,
for Your love would fill many oceans.
In token of the vows I have made before You,
I now take my cross and carry it, rejoicing, knowing that
You will never leave me nor forsake me; knowing that
You will be with me in sickness and in health,
to love and cherish me,
not only 'til death, but for all eternity."

I don't know what happened to the "chocolate-covered graham cracker" love note Randee handed to me on that rainy day down by the gymnasium. I must have lost it in one of our many moves. But I've read her love note to Him—the other Man in her life—many times. And her devotion to Him is so deep and sincere and loving that I am still in awe of her commitment.

"Many women do noble things,
but you surpass them all.
Charm is deceptive, and beauty is fleeting;
but a woman who fears the Lord is to be praised."

Proverbs 31:29-30

HOUSE CALLS

I BUMPED INTO HIM again this morning. I hadn't seen him in six years, and when I stopped for a cup of coffee at the neighborhood gas station, he was there too. It was so good to see him. Same friendly face. Same genuine smile — older with a few more wrinkles and a beard. But warm and open and . . . well, I'll tell you his story.

My secretary buzzed me to let me know he had called for an appointment to come in and talk. I reached for my appointment book and wrote his unfamiliar name in a slot. That particular day was already full of appointments. His name would go at the end of that list. I remember thinking I wouldn't have much left for him by the time I had seen all those other people. But I wrote his name in anyway.

On the day of his appointment, he walked into my office, and I was certain we had never met.

"Thanks for taking the time to see me, Pastor. I

know it's late in the afternoon, and you must have had a tiring day. I really appreciate the opportunity to get together." Such genuine sincerity from one who seemed to understand the rigors of pastoral life touched me. He was quiet and gentle. There were no *ums* or *ers* or *uhs* when he spoke. Every word was chosen carefully. Every thought expressed with measured precision.

He told me he had heard me speak a few Sundays before and wanted to come by to introduce himself. He was new to our area, and he wanted to come to our church. He also wanted to get more involved and thought that before he did, he should tell me his story. *Another storyteller,* I thought. My eyes looked straight into his, and I listened.

"I'm a former pastor. My wife and I have two daughters. They're teenagers, and they live with their mother. She and I have been divorced for about a year now." I sensed a profound sorrow in his voice. His hands were folded, but they weren't nervous hands. They were humble, unassuming hands, hands that sat quietly in his lap. There were no tears—only sorrow and scars as the storyteller remembered this chapter in his life. He paused for a moment and swallowed before continuing.

"I came home one day, and she told me she was leaving. I don't know if it was the pressure of the ministry or my failure as a husband or a general lack of communication. Probably some of all three. At any rate, she left two-and-a-half years ago, taking my two daughters with her."

This was a familiar story. As a pastor who minsters with single adults, I had heard it told by other storytellers, with different faces, at different times, in different locations. The storytellers all had different professions, different circumstances. Their stories all had different subplots and characters, but they told their stories with the same sorrow in each voice, the same ponderous pain.

"The first few weeks after they left were the most difficult of my life," he continued. "I never knew pain could be so profound. I resigned my church, not wanting to bring any more discredit to the ministry than I had already. But I underestimated how much I would miss the ministry. My wife was gone, my children were gone, and the ministry was gone, all in about three weeks."

It was quiet in my office. I was glad he was the last appointment of the day. I wanted to give this man enough time to tell his story.

"I seemed to wander for a few weeks. I knew I needed to find work so I took a job at a local furniture store. It was embarrassing for former parishoners to come in to the shop for furniture and find me there as a salesperson. They were gracious and made a difficult situation as painless as possible, but my life was bobbing up and down in some very deep water."

A determined smile came over his face. I've seen a variety of smiles people use for different occasions—one for happiness and pleasure, one when annoyed, and not wanting to seem too angry, one that is fake. But this man put on a determined smile designed to show bravery in the midst of a storm.

"Christmastime was the most difficult. In fact, Pastor, I was in crisis. One Saturday, late in the afternoon, I drove to the mall to buy a gift for my daughters. I walked up and down that mall, feeling suffocated. I don't even remember going into the department store. I only remember sort of 'coming to' as I stood in line to check out. I had two pairs of red, long john pajamas, but I couldn't remember why I was buying them or the town where my wife had moved. The cashier was very cordial. She said, 'Merry Christmas. Cash or charge?' All I could think to say was, 'I have no idea.' I left the pajamas sitting on the counter and walked out of the store and into the mall. I was near panic. I honestly believed I was going crazy, and I didn't know what to do."

Sometimes, when people tell me their stories, they get sidetracked with incidental details, things that don't add to the story. But this storyteller stayed with the essentials of his story.

"I sat outside on a bench for a long time. I looked into the eyes of people walking by, and wondered *Can you help me? I'm afraid I don't know what to do.* I watched mothers dragging children by the hand. I watched daddies shopping for gifts with their daughters. I listened to recorded Christmas carols. And I prayed for direction.

"I know that when things are really rough, it's good to do something nice for yourself. I've always loved books, so I decided to buy myself a book. I walked down to the bookstore and grabbed the first book I found."

The humble hands in this storyteller's lap helped him now, and he pretended to hold a book and open it. His eyes moistened, as he looked down at an imaginary volume and remembered the words:

"God, it's Saturday night and I feel like I'm bleeding to death on the inside. Ain't no way I'm gonna make it to church tomorrow. Do You make house calls?"

He looked up from his imaginary book and smiled at me. But it was not a smile of pleasure or relief. It was a smile of assurance, for my pastor face showed the pain of another's story, and my eyes were sad.

"As soon as I read those words, Pastor, I knew I was going to be all right, not because I felt better right then, but because I had been reminded that God does make house calls. I closed the book and walked straight over to the cashier. I took the book home, got in bed with that book and a flashlight, and I covered my head with the blankets. I turned on that flashlight and read that entire book. As I read, God began to help me with my anger and resentment and disappointment. I became convinced that He would meet me in the midst of my failure and sorrow."

I don't remember how our conversation ended that day. But seeing him again this morning, drinking coffee at the gas station, reminded me.

I wanted to mention his story just in case you're reading this book in bed, and you feel like crawling under the covers with a flashlight, and pulling the covers over your head—just in case it's Saturday night, and you can't see any way you'll make it to church tomorrow. Hold on, friend. Hold on because He still makes house calls.

> "Cast all your anxiety on Him
> because He cares for you."
>
> **1 Peter 5:7**

AIDS

HE CALLED ME last week, weeping and lonely and dying of AIDS. He said he used to go to a church like ours but hadn't been for years. Now that the doctors were telling him he had only a short time to live, he wanted to know if it would be all right if he attended a Sunday service.

He asked how long the service lasted. That was important because in his weakened condition, he could only be up for a couple of hours at a time. He asked about the seats, were they padded? Almost apologetically, he explained he had lost so much weight that it was difficult for him to sit on hard surfaces for any length of time.

Perhaps saddest of all, he asked about the people. Would they accept him the way he looked? Could he remain anonymous, sit in the back, not become a spectacle? He said he feared rejection, and if coming to church meant being rejected, he thought he'd be better off staying away.

I told him I'd rather answer his questions over lunch sometime, and we agreed to meet a couple of days later at a local eatery. He wasn't difficult to recognize when I walked into the restaurant. His skin was somewhat gray, with a touch of yellow seeping through. Thin, brittle hair. Hollowed eyes that were dark in bright daylight. I introduced myself to him, extending my hand. A strange thought entered my mind as I felt the bony cool of his touch. *You are the first,* I thought to myself. I have known for some time now that sooner or later, I would meet and minister to someone dying of AIDS. But he was the first.

We sat down and for a while we chatted about the day, what we had both been doing earlier, what to order for lunch. Soon, however, our conversation took on a more serious tone. I listened. He talked.

He talked of wrong choices and pain. He talked of broken relationships and sorrow. But most of all, he spoke of loneliness and solitude. He did not want to die alone. His daughter was to be married soon, and he was looking forward to helping her with the wedding. He only wished he was in better health, so he could do more.

There were moments in our conversation when tears fell onto the table. He was almost apologetic about his appearance, as he remembered the words of his doctor nearly two years before. "He told me I would have between eighteen and twenty-four months to live, if I took care of myself." He spoke in matter-of-fact tones, resolved to his own destiny.

"I grew up in a church like yours. I got married in a church like yours. I raised my kids and taught Sunday School and served as an usher on Sunday mornings in a church like yours. But I made some terribly wrong choices in my life — choices my wife and children didn't deserve. And now, I'm reaping what I sowed."

There was very little extraneous conversation. He seemed intent on sharing his life with me, and I tried to listen carefully. He pushed his barely touched plate of pasta out of the way, and with trembling hand, reached for his glass of ice water. After taking a small sip, he wiped his blue lips with a napkin and gazed out the window.

In music, it's called a grand pause — a moment in the middle of a piece when the music stops. That's what this man did. He took a *grand pause* to gather his composure before continuing.

Then he told me how sorry he was that he had left his wife and family seven years earlier. He told me he had confessed his sin and believed Christ had forgiven him. He wanted to spend his last days in church. Would it be OK if he came and sat in the back? People were often afraid of him, he said, and he didn't want to cause any trouble.

I hurt for this one who apologized for cluttering my life with his death. He would try to stay out of the way. He didn't want to make people feel uncomfortable. He would try not to act any sicker than absolutely necessary. Would it be all right if he just sat in the back, sang some of the songs, listened to the sermon, and . . . die?

I assured him that I would like him to come to our church.

I looked into his eyes, and I saw a man Christ died to save. I got angry in that restaurant. I was mad — mad at hell. And mad at myself for sending a message to anyone — sick or well — that implied God's house is only for those who aren't too sick.

How did we ever come to this place? We who are the church — how did we ever get so smug and comfortable and . . . *healthy* that we could send a message to the whores and pimps and thieves and homosexuals of this world that says, "This is not a place for people who are as sick as you. You're unclean, you're as good as dead, you're already starting to smell. Even the Resurrection can't help you, so don't mess up the clean sheets in this hospital."

"Jesus wept."

John 11:35

THE VIEW FROM
THE TOP

DURING MY TEEN years, I watched with great interest the construction of the St. Louis Gateway Arch, a wicket-shaped monument built to memorialize Lewis and Clark's expedition that opened up the West to development and exploration. The construction was amazing, each side of the structure rising independent of the other, leaning legs that gradually tilted toward the center. Higher and higher the two sides rose, 200, 300, 400, and more. Finally, the last piece of the puzzle was placed, the top section that connected the two segments, more than 600 feet above the banks of the Mississippi River.

Several months after the last piece was positioned, the National Park Service held a grand opening, allowing the public to ride the elevator to the top of the Arch. I decided to ride to the top. But I wanted more—I wanted to be the *first* to ride to the top.

My brother and I invited two other friends to join us for the great event. Nine o'clock in the morning was the scheduled grand opening. We decided to arrive the night before and spend the night in the parking lot. We were all willing to wait the several hours necessary to guarantee our place in history as the first people to ride to the top of the Gateway Arch.

Rain pelted the car roof as we sat in the parking lot—slow and rythmic, the rain droned. The windows of the car soon fogged up, as the four of us talked about life and other serious matters like baseball and girls and what it would be like to ride to the top of the Arch. We talked about the Mississippi River and the barges that traveled its waters. We talked of other friends and vacations, and food. It was talking about food that started our decline.

Hamburgers in particular were a favorite topic. How good a hamburger would taste. Maybe with cheese? And some fries and a chocolate shake. There weren't any other cars in the parking lot, and we thought aloud, *What could it hurt? We'll go get something to eat and then come back. We won't lose our place in line because there isn't any line. We're the only ones here.*

Within moments, we pulled out of the parking lot and started our search for the closest place for a burger. St. Louis is a big town with lots of eateries, but most of them close around midnight. We were determined, however, and finally came upon a greasy-spoon that was open all night.

One-thirty in the morning. That's what time it was when we got our food. We each ate two cheeseburgers, fries and a chocolate shake, then we drove back across town to the parking lot of the Gateway Arch to take our place in destiny. We resumed our conversations about baseball and girls and the Mississippi River. The rain continued its drone on the roof like a hypnotic symphony — soft, soothing rhythms. With our tummies full of burgers we were soon too tired to hold our heads up. We tried to sleep sitting up and leaning our heads against the windows, but it was much too crowded.

There was simply no comfortable way we could sleep, but our bodies cried out for sleep. Before long, someone suggested that riding to the top of the Arch would be fun, all right, but maybe we didn't have to be the *first*. Maybe we should just plan to come back sometime the next day.

We were too sleepy to deliberate this question at length — the decision was unanimous. Abandon ship and forget this silly idea about being the first to ride to the top of the Gateway Arch. We headed home and by 3:30 we were counting sheep.

I remember watching the evening news the following day. All the local stations sent news teams to cover the opening of the Arch. And they interviewed him. The guy who was first in line to ride to the top. Every single one of the local stations had that guy's face plastered across the screen.

"How'd you like the view from up there?" one of the anchor people asked. "A million-dollar view," he said. "I think it was just beautiful, and I'm glad I did it."

I missed it. I could have done it, but I traded a bag full of burgers and a warm bed for a chance to make history.

So did they; the twelve guys who followed Him around.

It had been a long day. In fact, the three years they had followed the Carpenter had been *filled* with long days. He had gathered them for supper, broke bread, and shared wine. They were all together, and it was nice. It seemed a little strained, this supper, like it was their last. He talked as though this might be the last time they'd be together like this.

They didn't understand. Why was He so serious? What made Him so somber?

They finished the meal, sang a chorus, and left. They went to a favorite spot, a garden—a place called Gethsemane. It was dark and quiet and a perfect place for prayer. The disciples were tired and full. Maybe they couldn't think of what to pray, or maybe the thought of prayer didn't occur to any of them. But it occurred to Him.

"Wait here. I'm going off a little way to pray."

They didn't mean to. It's just that their bellies were full of wine and bread. The meal they had made them sleepy, more sleepy than they could fight. They didn't sleep long. But they slept long enough to miss an opportunity of a lifetime.

I wonder what they would have heard? What did His groaning and travail sound like? If they had stayed awake, what would they have felt as they heard the Lord of all praying for them? They had the opportunity to share in one of the most incredible events the world will ever know. If they could only have waited, wide awake, with the Lamb of God. They could have watched Jesus pray on bended knee. Quite a sight—an inside perspective reserved only for those who will wait on Him.

Of course you and I still have a chance. He's invited us to join Him at the top of the "mountain of prayer," a standing invitation to walk into His presence. But we have to decide. *I* have to decide that the view from the top is worth the wait. What He wants is someone who will wait on Him, hear His heart for the world, hear His voice asking for intimacy and fellowship with men and women. His great desire is to reveal Himself to those who will take advantage of a secluded, quiet time with Him. Those who make the effort are treated to a spectacular view of God . . . and life.

> "My soul waits for the Lord
> more than watchmen wait for the morning,
> more than watchmen wait for the morning."
>
> **Psalm 130:6**

IF I COULD TELL YOU

I KNOW MANY STORIES — old and new, happy and sad. And if I could, I would tell them to you. But if I told them, I would be revealing what was spoken in confidence.

I could tell you of people I see nearly every day who lean bravely into the wind of life and sail against the tide, close to the rocks of disappointment and failure, in perilous proximity to the breakers of broken dreams. If I could, I would share with you some of the insecurities and doubts that plague many of the people I love and care for. But in the telling, I would only deepen those insecurities. Many people tell me their personal stories. I know things I dare not repeat. I'm restrained by a trust. To violate that trust would be unforgivable.

And so, I will not tell you all the stories I know. But I will tell you one more.

He was funny. He loved to laugh and joke and

watch others respond to his zany antics. Even as a young child, he had learned that people like to laugh, and he enjoyed making that happen. Now, at fifteen, he was the high school class clown. But deep within, he harbored an emptiness, a longing to be fulfilled, a nagging, gnawing need for significance that never left him. And he didn't know why.

But he leaned into the wind and sailed on.

One day, in ninth-grade English, Miss Michaeloff took the large text of classic writings from its place on her desk and began class.

"Today we're going to read Emily Dickinson."

She opened the book and read—slowly, with deep feeling, in whispered tones and unashamed truthfulness, the words of a young woman; words of another mariner leaning into the wind:

> *"I'm Nobody! Who are you?*
> *Are you—Nobody—Too?*
> *Then there's a pair of us?*
> *Don't tell! they'd advertise—you know!"*

He sat in class, listening to Miss Michaeloff. But he could not look at her. She was peering into his soul, and he feared detection. If he looked up, she might wonder why his eyes were so sad. She might realize that the words she read verbalized the deep questions in his life. She might ask what he thought. And he didn't know what he thought. She might ask him to comment, and he had no comment — only questions, and a realization that the story she read was his. He was a *nobody,* and he came to that realization as he sat in honor's English class on a warm, spring afternoon.

When the bell rang for class to be dismissed, he walked out the door and down the crowded hall; he did not laugh or smile or even speak to those who hurried past him. He thought. He pondered. He recited the first line of Emily's verse to himself, as he looked into the eyes of his classmates: *I'm Nobody. Who are you?*

And he leaned into the wind and sailed on.

For days and weeks and months he sailed, leaning into the wind of life, noticing the crowded sealanes — noticing the other mariners around him, their empty vessels sliding in and out of lonely ports-of-call, barely afloat, afraid. He watched and listened to others who covered their lonely lives with laughter. He helped them with their laughter. He was funny. But deep inside, where they could not see, he recited Emily's poem to himself, and he cried, *I'm Nobody. Who are you?*

Weeping silently to himself, he leaned into the wind and sailed on.

One day, the young man noticed a storm on the horizon of his life. He had seen other storms. He knew from experience that when storms come, you have to prepare for them. So he pulled in his sails; he secluded himself, and battened-down his life tightly so the storm could not harm him.

But there seemed to be no safe harbor. The storm surged. The darkness overwhelmed. The wind howled like never before, and he was afraid. Wave upon wave of sorrow and doubt washed over his life. Fear pounded his deck. He leaned into the wind with all his might, but he could not sail on. He silently cried out in fear, *Help. I need somebody to help me. My name is Nobody, and I need help.*

That's when he saw *Him,* standing brave and unafraid on the mountainous waves of doubt and fear. His voice was a thunderous symphony, soaring over the noise of the storm; His smile, gentle as a spring breeze, and in His hand, a bough of peace pointed the way toward safe passage. This Mariner of mercy looked into the face of *Nobody* and spoke three wonderful words: "Peace, Be still!"

No storm could threaten in His presence, and in submission and obedience, the waves subsided and the wind returned to the four corners of the earth. This Captain brought with Him safe passage and friendship and loyalty and love. "These are for you," He said to the *Nobody.* "I bought and paid for them with *My* life. Now, I give them to you."

The young man reached out and humbly accepted the generous offer. He listened, as the Giver of every good and perfect gift spoke again. "There is healing and forgiveness in My name. There is eternal life and purpose in My name. You, who once were *Nobody* are now adopted by a King, and I give you a new name: *Christian.* It means *one who follows Christ.*"

"When you feel alone or afraid, remember Me and My eternal covenant with all who will call upon My name. When you feel insignificant, inadequate, inferior, remember My promise. I will never leave you or forsake you. And when storms of uncertainty and loneliness appear on the horizon remember *your* name, for in remembering *your* name, you remember *My* name. Never speak of *Nobody* again."

"God . . . gave Him the name
that is above every name,
that at the name of Jesus
every knee should bow,
in heaven and on earth and under the earth,
and every tongue confess that Jesus Christ is Lord,
to the glory of God the Father."

Philippians 2:9-11

"In the night I remember Your name, O Lord."

Psalm 119:55